Deben

Because of Colorful Doors

A trilogy of a globetrotter's
adventures through
Scotland, England and Cuba

Deleen Wills

This book is a trio of nonfiction travel tales.

Copyright © 2017 DFWills Publishing

Printed by Createspace

ISBN-13:
978-1548187262

ISBN-10:
1548187267

Second Edition

If you have any comments or questions, please contact Deleen Wills through Facebook at Behind Colorful Doors or deleenwills@gmail.com

Cover Photo by Deleen Wills

DEDICATION & THANKS

To my aunts who encouraged me to explore the world, dream big and experience life. Sadly, all are no longer with me but each heard about my adventures. They are: Ardie, Colleen, Helen, Joyce and Patti.

SINCERE THANKS TO:

Beth E. Pitcher	Copy Editor
Joyce Gleason	Proofreader
Jessica R. M. Spurrier	Cover Design and Deleen Wills Portrait
NiCole Anderson	Interior Design

ACKNOWLEDGMENTS

Because of Colorful Doors is a collaborative effort and my deepest appreciation goes out to my very patient and loving family and friends who encouraged me to continue writing and sharing more travel escapades. They include but are not limited to:

Beth E. Pitcher, for expertly and patiently copy-editing the stories and allowing me to bounce all kinds of thoughts by her. A dear friend who I would never know if we hadn't met in an elevator in Quito, Ecuador before our Galapagos expedition—serendipity at its finest.

Jon D. Pitcher, for his expertise in British-isms and English grammar.

Joyce Gleason, for lending her talents in proof-reading, sharing her opinions, laughter, moral support and being such a grand travel-mate.

NiCole Anderson, for her talent with technology, crafting the interior design, and for being such a loyal and trusted friend.

Jessica R. M. Spurrier, jacket designer, photographer, graphic designer, artist and friend. See her work at www.greengateimages.etsy.com.

Pearl Aldridge, for her years of friendship since those early Mansfield College days.

Joyce Townsley, our Scotland tour guide extraordinaire and lifetime friend.

Mark Wills, for his ongoing exceptional patience helping with technology issues.

To my cheerleaders for their continued encouragement: J. Steven Hunt, artist, writer and long-time friend. And those who have continued to ask, "When is your next book coming out?" Annette, Beth, Carol, Doug, Heather, Jeannie, Joan, Joyce, Michelle, Nancy, NiCole, Sue, Suzanne, my parents Del and Patty Riley, and many readers of *Behind Colorful Doors*.

Contents

1 The Kaleidoscope of Colorful Doors   1

2 The Walnut Door   98

3 The Blue and White Door   179

Take a seat—I have a few stories to share with you.

Kaleidoscope of Colorful Doors

How It All Began

Road Rage and Meltdown

Fourteen miles seemed like fifty on a sunshiny July day in 1996. We'd only just left Oxford University in our rented compact blue Peugeot with orange license plate. Fortunately, it didn't broadcast the big "L" we'd seen on the back of many cars in England. It meant "L" for "Learner" but I thought for us, it might be "L" for "Loser."

As co-pilot, my sole responsibility was to let my husband Mark, our designated driver, know which road off the roundabouts we'd take. After trying to figure out the English roadway system and signage, I'd had it. "Stop the car now!" I demanded, unbuckling the seatbelt, ready to climb out even before coming to a complete stop at the side of a country road. We'd decided to take the scenic route driving to Scotland and stay off the motorway for the time being. Maybe not our best decision.

The pathetic thing was I had studied up on roundabouts and therefore I thought that I was mentally prepared. I knew the first had been installed in 1909 in Letchwood Garden City, an ancient parish of Hertfordshire (shires are like our counties) in northern England. I *knew* when we entered a roundabout, called an "approach leg," that it would be important to yield. I *knew* we would be circling counterclockwise and we'd be in the outside lane for

1

exiting. I *knew* we could safely stay in the inner lane, looping, until we figured out where to exit. I *knew* there could be an approach nose to the splitter island (read it in a booklet on driving tips for the U.K but have no idea what it is), maybe a sidewalk, and should there be a pedestrian crossing, we'd have to stop. I *knew* it all—or so I thought.

The initial trauma started just outside Oxford where we encountered the first roundabout and circled round and round and round and round, yes, four times, before exiting on the road that sounded most correct. What I hadn't discovered in my reading prior to attempting the first fiasco was that the signage on the roundabouts didn't post the towns we wanted to get to. At home, if traveling from Seattle, Washington south on Interstate 5, one would read, Tacoma, Portland, Salem, Albany, Eugene. Turns out in England, it shows the last town—like Eugene, not helpful at all when trying to locate a town only twenty miles away.

The ornamentation in the center island that we saw four times appeared to be the only highlight of the first roundabout drama. In the middle sat a sizeable topiary in the shape of a hefty swan surrounded by other bushes. Or so I thought. Apparently, I'd been the only one to see the swan as others only saw uneven bushes and shrubs. And I had no proof of the remarkable centerpiece since I didn't take a photo due to being preoccupied with matters at hand. I also had read that on the central island of a roundabout it would showcase its own distinct personality, making it one-of-a-kind. Expecting to see all roundabouts with islands of mini-gardens, fountains, sculptures, memorials, giant bugs, birds and animals, and tributes to monarchy, I didn't realize we'd see mostly bushes, shrubs and weeds. I felt frazzled enough after the first go-round—and with sweaty palms, coming up all too quickly—the dreaded second roundabout. I tried to amaze my traveling trio with roundabout terminology and informed them we were entering the approach leg. It didn't seem to impress my husband and each time we did a complete circle, and he asked, "Which road do we take?" Each loop his same question sounded a little louder. I tried to make light of the situation by pointing out what looked like giant butterflies in the center of the circle. "Those are scraggly bushes again," I heard from the back seat. After looping around this circle three times and even more exasperated, we exited onto a road toward a town that sounded familiar. That's when I tossed the maps and gladly turned navigation over to Martha. With a sigh of relief, I hopped in the back seat.

Once we decoded this highway peculiarity, new navigator Martha efficiently wrote on a sheet of paper the town names for the road off the roundabout that we needed to find and exit. For the rest of the week, she and Mark would do this charting process each night before launching the next day. I steered clear of them. Our sapphire rental car had a speedometer shown in both miles and kilometers, with the miles printed in larger numbers. We knew that the speed limit of 30 miles per hour converted to 48 kilometers per hour. Speeding right along at 70 miles per hour really became a whopping 112 in kilometers per hour. I felt thrilled to be done with the responsibility, anxiety and pressure of being co-pilot.

Since I am directionally challenged, I prefer to watch the scenery go by. I had done an unofficial poll over the years and those of us who are afflicted with this malady, wonder, when trying to decipher a map, why it's always printed upside down.

Preparation for Embarkation

I not only felt grateful but enthusiastic for this journey because road-trippers and traveling buddies, Martha from Boston, and Nina from Oregon, were embarking on this lark with us. They had travelled with us before on a whirlwind trip around Europe, so we knew they were hearty stock and up for this adventure. Our dinky fuel-efficient, manual trans-mission with gear-shift-in-the-opposite-direction rental car, now nicknamed the Bluebird of Happi-ness, had been efficiently packed ready to roll. We were scrunched but opted for this vehicle category due to gas prices equivalent to $6 per gallon. I'd heard some people refer to driving the roadway system in Great Britain as "driving on the wrong side of the road." It's never "wrong" when you're in someone else's country.

There were four different-colored Rick Steves' *Europe Through the Back Door* bags, one for each of us, safely stowed in the boot (our trunk). A trunk to the British is a large, old-fashioned suitcase. We'd learned to pack light under Rick's sage tutelage, plus we trusted his books full of advice from his years of travel around the world. Each time he came to speak in our area, we'd go listen and learn.

He became my travel guru and we not only adopted his philosophy of packing but that of travel.

I really appreciated one of his quotes, "Ideally, travel broadens our perspectives personally, culturally, and politically. Suddenly, the palette with which we paint the story of our lives has more colors." This heartened and fortified my wanderlust—a strong desire for or impulse to wander or travel and explore the world. It had been instilled in me at an early age by my parents as our family of five traipsed around the Pacific Northwest camping in our fifteen-foot travel trailer.

Our chauffeur for the week seemed mentally prepared to drive on the opposite side of the road. When riding back and forth several days into London from Oxford University the week before, my husband sat behind the bus driver observing and soaking in the highway vibes. He didn't know the manual gear shift would also be in the opposite direction. He did know he'd be driving for the first time through English countryside to Scotland, the birthplace of my mother's grandfather and centuries of relatives before him. We were chasing down my Scottish roots. I'd heard about "bonnie" (meaning nice or pretty) Scotland all my life and I look Celtic with light blonde hair growing up, fair complexion and blue eyes. I dreamed of visiting Scotland one day.

Lebanon, Oregon—pronounced Leb-a-nun, not Leb-a-non, like the country, is where my life began. I enlightened my car-mates that my mother was born in Bloomington, Nebraska in 1926. Her mother was born eighteen miles away, in Alma, Nebraska in 1896. Mom told me her grandfather, Thomas, was born in 1848 in Sanquhar, Scotland, pronounced "sankur." I read that this area is really considered the Lowlands, and not too far across the border from England. It is a very small town on the River Nith in Dumfries and Galloway. The Saint Bride's church cemetery contains memorials to my family and the ruins of Sanquhar Castle stand nearby. I could hardly wait to get there. I didn't want to confuse them too much so explained for now the *Reader's Digest* condensed version of the family history. My great-great-great grandfather, William Lorimer (#1), and his son, my great-great grandfather, William (#2), lived in the castle and my great grandfather, Thomas Lorimer, was born there. To explain, William #1 was appointed by royalty as overseer of the Sanquhar castle and land, located in the lowlands of Scotland in the late 1700s. My great grandpa, Thomas Lorimer, was born in that same castle in 1848. He was around fifteen years old when his mother died. Though the new castle was being built a short distance away, his father (William #2) was getting too old for the job. It was time to move on. The old castle was sold to a private party. Costly to maintain, it changed hands once again. Due to neglect and age, the castle fell into ruins. In 1872, father (William #2), age sixty-four, and son Thomas, age twenty-four, left Scotland, moved to America and settled in Nebraska.

Further educating them, I shared my geography lesson that Scotland is around one-third the size of Oregon, about the size of South Carolina, and all of Great Britain actually would fit inside our state of Oregon with about 8,000 miles to spare. Glasgow, where we weren't going, is the biggest city with Edinburgh coming in second. Our climate is drizzlingly similar and the countryside is much like the same garden look we have in Oregon. When looking at a map, Anchorage, Alaska is similar in latitude to the northernmost Shetland Islands, much farther north. Scotland also has almost eight hundred islands with about one hundred thirty inhabited. Lesson over...for now.

Even though I thought they'd heard enough about my family, Martha asked a couple of questions that led me back to sharing more about my heritage. My great-great-grandmother, Jean Wightman, died in 1853 at age forty-six. She left a broken-hearted husband, William (#2), and eight children.

In March 1872, father and son travelled on foot with a few belongings sixty miles to the west coast of Scotland and boarded the steamship, Anglia. She accommodated one hundred first class passengers, eighty intermediate class and seven hundred in steerage class. Those in steerage were required to provide their own mattresses, bedding and mess kits (plate, mug, knife, fork, spoon and water can). I suspect they were in steerage with most other immigrants. It sailed out of Fort Glasgow headed south down the Firth of Clyde. I wondered how they felt as they watched their homeland disappear in the mist, perhaps one with regret and the other with excitement. They came to New York on March 29, 1872, and on the passenger list they were described as farmers.

They began a cross-country train journey westward and settled in Harlan County, Nebraska. I read excerpts to my travelling companions and told them that the misspelled words are from a two-page letter that became part of the family chronicles.

William wrote to his chum, James, back in Scotland dated 9th June 1872 from Nebraska:

"I was very sick for the first week and vowed I would never cross the seas for love or money again. I laugh at that now. We got to New York on the 29th and I made up my mind that it is a meanest place I ever saw. Some of the by-streets were over two feet deep with dirt. I was a little over 24 hours in it and I was not sorry to leave it by the Pennsylvania Railroad. We arrived in Pittsburgh on the afternoon of the thirty-first after staying there for a little over thirty minutes we were again on the road for Chicago, where we landed on the morning of first the April. Everything miserable this far and Chicago with its burned streets and knee deep in dirt was not very cheery sight. I was a little over one hour in Chicago and I saw nothing in it to wish myself back there again.

After leaving it everything improved as if by magic the prairie that you see leaving Chicago improves very mile for you till you are at Lincoln. We stayed 3 days in Lincoln looking for land and I found it very difficult to get if there is no one ahead of you that will take some interest in a person. They will find it a very hard job to get with land. I tried Adams County and a good many more but all the lands were taken up that is land without wood and watter and even most of either with or without those advantages. I spent ten days looking out for land and my board was 2 dollars a day. That was near one pound per day for the two of us and if you went fifty miles by rail you had to pay 3 or 4 dollars a peace it cost me quite a little pile of money before I got settled here but we have got 320 acres which I mean to pay the government price for. We have plenty of wood and watter. I have broken six acres and I have not seen a stone the size of my hand in it.

Today I happened to be 20 miles east of this and had such a storm as you never saw in the middle of as hott a day as ever we have in Scotland. The sky clouded over and right in the winds eye I thought it was going off to leave me all right. I watched its course for half an hour and at best was painfully aware that I must look alive or get the full benefit of it. I had my team with me and we were loaded but I put them to it full trot for a house I saw some distance ahead of me. I got forward and unhitched them from my wagon before I got a drop. I had 20 yards to go to make the stable when I got there I was perfectly soaked. I could not make the house again. The pieces of ice that were falling were fully larger than a nutt. I was thurtsy and I lifted m hand and ate some of them. They were pure ice. The Miscatoes are very bad on us just now but they don't last very long. You may some idea of hard I am working when I tell that I have known of a hird of several thousand buffalo being within 20 miles of here and I have not yet payed them a visit though they have been near us. I have shot nothing. I have shot a lone antelope and missed. I came home and selected a tree about the same distance and put a bullet within 4 inches of the object, aimed at it, was a small piece of bark taken from the centre of it. I have killed one porcupine one skunk and bagers one of them I broke my fathers staff over its head. We have small turkeys some rabbits some hares geece grouce ducks and very large variety of small birds of many plumages.

...We have a good climate for fruits there is a very good variety of wild fruits growing along banks of our streams. I am afraid that our selection of fish here is very poor and they are very ugly quite a disjust to handle them. I expect that we will have a post office within 4 miles by the time I get an answer from you and a railroad in two years if not sooner. I would like if you could come. You can get your land for nothing and provisions are as dear as they are in the old country...

The house I have got is partly dugout and part bluff. Before we had it finished the rain rained and softened the ground and the house fell and early (one morning when we were in our beds, 3 oclock) broke my fathers arm the same evening when I got up my mulls had gone off...No more at present.

With sinsere regards I remain your affect Chum Tom Lorimer."

Father and son shared in the responsibility of homesteading three hundred and ten acres, each farming the land together.

My great-great-grandfather only survived another three years, dying on October 28, 1875. His son buried him on the Nebraska prairie on foreign soil in two tartans, the patterns were Stewart and Wallace. No one knows for sure why two were used. The Stewart Clan motto is "Courage grows strong at a wound." The tartan is red with navy and green creating the plaid print. The Wallace Clan motto is "For liberty." The tartan color varies and I can't determine why. There is red Wallace, green Wallace and blue Wallace.

But why had he been buried in two tartans? This piqued my interest and upon further research I discovered that the Lorimer family was actually not entitled to wear the Scottish tartan since only a Highland Scot could sport the tartan. As Lowlanders because of where Sanquhar is located, the Lorimers simply were not eligible to wear a tartan. As it turned out, however, any loyal subject of the Crown could wear the Royal Stewart tartan. That explained the Stewart Tartan but not the Wallace; well, except for family lore that will be explained later.

Our Sanquhar visit would be at the end of our Scottish adventure. Using our paper version of MapQuest directions, Mark drove us safely adapting quickly to driving on the other side of the road. I felt beyond ecstatic to get to Scotland but it would be a least a six-hour drive to our destination at a B&B in Edinburgh.

After the first roundabout fiasco on the A34 we turned west onto the A40 and the second infamous roundabout at B4449. That's when I gave up and turned over the co-pilot duties to Martha. I had quickly regained my composure and returned to my normal calm self by the time we drove through the charming villages of Burford and Northleach, skirting around the enchanting Cotswolds. On the M6 we went by Stoke-on-Trent, speeding along with lorries (trucks) that looked like mini-versions of our too-long and too-big semi-trucks, familiar looking cars with different names and many families towing their recreational vehicles. By now, Manchester was to the east with Liverpool to the west, situated on the River Mersey.

Reading these recognizable names, especially the River Mersey, caused us to remember and almost simultaneously break out into our own rendition of an oldie but goodie song with husband Mark playing thumb drums on the steering wheel. We belted out *Ferry Cross the Mersey*, written by a guy named Gerry in England in the 60s then made popular later in the United States by his singing group named Gerry and the Pacemakers. Singing loudly and slightly off-key in our best à capella voices, we tried to recall the lyrics, stumbling through a line or two. Was it "hearts tossed, turned or thrown in every way"? When we got to another line it was something like, "we don't care what your name is … " and half of our quartet sang "boy" but two of us emphasized "girl." We hummed, mumbled, slurred and lalalalala'd but we all came together on the "ferry 'cross the Mersey" part.

We were somewhat pleased with ourselves for remembering most of the words. To this day when I hear this song on the oldies station, it immediately teleports me twenty years back to our road trip through England to Scotland. We were also aware that the Beatles began their musical careers in Liverpool but we weren't here for song and dance. We were on a mission to get to Scotland. Munching on cookies called biscuits and potato chips called crisps, we followed the M6 through Yorkshire, seeing stone houses, limestone hills, green pastureland and stone walls separating farmers' properties. From a distance, we could see a field that appeared blanketed in white. It turned out to be a moor covered in tall, white blooming flowers that looked like the puffy white cotton balls that I'd seen in the southern part of the U.S.

Reaching Carlisle, we unanimously agreed to exit the motorway to see a more scenic route so we jumped off onto the A7 dual carriageway that would also lead us right into Edinburgh and our B&B. The road seemed empty compared to the motorway and much more peaceful. At Houghton, we stopped at Hadrian's Wall monument. Some people mistake the Wall as the border between England and Scotland. It is not but the border isn't far. The Wall marks one of the frontiers of the Roman Empire. It runs from the Solway Firth on the Irish Sea on the west across northern England to the banks of the River Tyne near the North Sea on the east coast. It had been built as a defensive fortification which began in 1022 AD in the reign of the emperor Hadrian. Nina read aloud the information sign which informed us that it totaled eighty-six miles and we were standing at mile sixty-four. We viewed photos of the Wall going over berms, around hills, by castles now ruins, over streams, through green countryside, brown land and still visible in most areas. After stretching our legs, we were back in our Bluebird viewing panoramas of pastures in low rolling green hills spotted with dairy and angus cows and cute sheep with black faces, separated by dark green rows of hedges, bushes or stone fences. Occasionally a quaint-looking home would have a brightly painted door, many red. Motoring through the little village of Longtown, with only two miles to the little hamlet of Carwinley, I knew we were almost to the border of Scotland. Looking at the map, the border seemed to cut across the countryside, zigzagging upwards also using the River Elk as the boundary. For some reason, it reminded me of an uneven hem on a dress I tried making in seventh grade.

Bonnie Scotland

About two o'clock that afternoon we pulled off the road amongst the purple heather and lanky thistle, and took a picture of the big blue sign with white printing, "Welcome to SCOTLAND" with a white X centered in a box at the top. On one side of the road were grazing Scottish blackface sheep, oblivious to tourists, and on the other side was the ambling River Esk, appearing not to be in any hurry to go anywhere. I expected or hoped for a border-crossing building or a shack, or I'd settle for a hut, where we'd get our passports stamped or at the very least, a "Welcome "or "Fàilte" (pronounced fall-cheh) in Scots Gaelic. No such luck with the warm welcome to my homeland. Nor a Scottish man dressed in a kilt playing, *Scotland the Brave* on bagpipes. My bubble burst a little.

However, standing there at the border, my heart started thudding against my chest and my eyes overflowed with tears. I couldn't explain to my fellow travelers why this happened so I didn't even try. Martha gave me a big hug like she understood. Her heritage was Irish and we felt a Celtic sisterhood because I had some Irish in me too, as my father's grandfather and grandmother came from Ireland. Finally, I stood in one of the countries of my forefathers (and foremothers). Two other countries where my "great-greats" came from are Ireland and Norway. I would get to those countries in the future, by golly.

Two miles into Scotland we passed the picturesque March Bank Country House and continued through burghs like Langholm, where the River Esk and Ewes Water (like a stream) meet. Driving on High Street, the only main road, we passed a white steeple church and town hall. In the distance, we could see on a little hillside a tall obelisk, obviously a memorial for someone important. We climbed in elevation to the hamlet of Arkleton, which seemed to be just a stone mansion on an estate. The pleasant community of Teviothead, at just over nine hundred feet elevation, is on the River Teviot with a parish church and not much more. A burgh, we determined, was a small settlement with several dozen homes and a church. A hamlet might be church-less with just a few homes.

The land flattened out through Branxholme, and after Hawick we crossed Ettrick Water. Also flattened out was a once living little creature now a pancake on the road. I didn't look too closely but it didn't appear to have been a bunny or squirrel. Looking over the side of the bridge we saw that the water color looked periwinkle. A mother merganser and seven babies floated along not caring that we were watching them. Momma merganser had a brown head with some auburn tones and feathers poked out from the back of her head like she was having a bad hair day. Two of her black and white brood climbed up on her back and were hitching a ride and as she swam towards the reeds, her ducklings paddled as fast as they could to keep up. My new word for this trip was "birdorable."

The road headed up the valley of the River Teviot. The river appeared at low level and in most places, I bet we could have walked across. Blackface sheep roamed freely and with open range, we all watched carefully for them and other wildlife, as deer were plentiful. We saw a small herd of reddish-colored deer, munching on grass in the distance. They were good size and we discovered they are the biggest deer in the country. The emerald low rolling hills and scenery didn't change drastically. My husband mentioned it appeared to be a perfect fly fishing river and wondered why he didn't see anyone. He'd been an avid fly fisherman since childhood and knew a potentially good fishing hole when he saw it. The Strath Errick, actually a tributary, poured into the River Tweed that we crossed and paralleled for some miles.

What changed often were the clouds. White puffy light ones to thicker gray were common in short periods of time. I concluded that the Scottish weather would be difficult to predict. Clouds moved quickly across the sky creating distinctive profiles and silhouettes with their shadows making unique figures on the ground. One white cloud had a dark center looking like an angel blowing a horn. The shadow on the ground looked more like a miniature horse.

We could tell we were getting closer to Edinburgh (pronounced Eh-din-bur-uh) because of more traffic and several well-manicured golf courses. Roundabouts were beginning to be more frequent and, once again, I thanked Martha for taking over this daunting responsibility. The River Tweed veered east and we followed the Gala Water which parallels the A7 heading north, going by Fountainhall and across the Gore Water on Shank Bridge. Just past Lothian Bridge, restaurants, homes and businesses lined both sides of the street; we were in the burbs of Edinburgh.

I'd done plenty of pre-trip research on Edinburgh and informed my traveling trio what we could expect to see and experience: The castle, Holyrood Palace and the Royal Mile with lots of memorials, statues and churches. I shared that the city had been founded prior to the 7th century AD, and is the capital, located on the southern shore of the Firth of Forth. It is the home to the Scottish Parliament and the seat of the monarchy. The University of Edinburgh was founded in 1582 and is one of the four universities in the city. I worked at a local university and it interested me to see what other universities were like. If we visited a campus, I always bought a pencil with the university name on it at their bookstore. That seemed enough info for now. The next day we'd start with the Hop On/Hop Off bus to get an overview of the city.

Martha, reading directions to Mark, delivered us competently to Ravensneuk Guest House on Blacket Avenue, right off Dalkeith Road. I found this Bed-and-Breakfast not on the worldwide web, which being just a few years old hadn't proven itself trustworthy yet, but instead by making inquiries and receiving brochures in the mail. Each time I got a packet of information it seemed like Christmas with something new to read. I'd been working on this trip of discovery for over a year.

The brochure described our B&B as, "A refined accommodation in a friendly family atmosphere." It included gourmet breakfast, proudly boasted itself as a non-smoking establishment, plus it had parking. When we pulled up, I noticed on one side of the house a large bay window. I hoped our room would be on the first or second floor in a three-sided, window room.

We were welcomed by a woman with a warm smile and a heavy accent. I really felt like I was in a foreign country now, especially when someone spoke English and I could hardly understand her. After registering, we easily carried our one bag each as we were escorted to our rooms, up three flights of a spiral staircase with burgundy plush carpet and a white rose in the middle of each step, so plush I sank down about an inch with each footstep. It seemed a step back in time to the 1950s or 60s.

We entered our room and happily for me it had a bay window. It appeared complete with a lumpy double-size bed, sink in the corner, towels hanging on a wooden rack and steam heat billowing from the clanging pipes, even though it was July. A red plaid shade sat on top of the lamp in the middle of the round nightstand. I knew it must be their clan tartan. In the middle of the bay window sat a wooden vanity with two drawers on each side and a three-way mirror. The same red plaid that matched the lamp-shade covered the padded stool. There were two overstuffed rust-colored, velvet cloth chairs. En-croaching to half of the windows were heavy cloth material curtains in a lighter shade of rust, more like a murky orange. The compact en-suite bathroom seemed efficient with a sink, toilet and tall shower.

After my earlier roundabout trauma, admirable recovery, scenic drive and now euphoria of being in another new country (and that of my roots), we reflected a few minutes as we sat and sank down into the 1950s-looking chairs. We felt a little like a queen and king, especially after accommodations in a college dorm at Mansfield College in Oxford for the past ten days.

It seemed a good time to stretch our legs so we headed to the main part of the city about a three-mile stroll through neighborhoods. This is always one of my favorite things while travelling, viewing different architecture in homes and buildings and hoping to encounter some locals. We were greeted with head nods, and one man asked if he could help us find anything in particular. I enjoyed listening to his Scottish brogue even though he spoke quickly and I

19

could hardly understand him. He spoke English but it wasn't like any English I'd heard before. We told him we were famished and our proprietors told us that their favorite restaurant was The Doric Tavern on Market Street. He said, "Aye" pronounced "Eye" meaning yes, they were correct, we'd have a delicious meal. He said we had about a twenty-minute walk to go. His parting words of advice were, "You might wish to have the sticky toffee pudding, it's lovely." I'd never heard food called lovely before. We always said food tasted yummy or delicious.

Wandering down the street we came upon a cottage painted all white with a bright red front door complete with a gold door knocker and matching mail slot and handle. Around the corner sat a stone two-story home with a stone fence around the backyard. Part of the fence had an arch and a blotchy, faded green door that appeared partially open. I peeked in and it revealed a garden chock-full of flowers, two wooden benches, a water fountain and several trees. Branches of the trees stretched out like long arms gently holding several birdhouses. Another strikingly red front door, #21, indicated on the tile along the street, was flanked by ferns trailing down both sides. Magically, a breeze caught the rounded wooden door at the side of the home, and ever so slightly, the door opened enough to expose a courtyard with a pebbled, curving pathway leading to somewhere I couldn't see. I decided it would be best if I didn't trespass but it certainly tempted me. I'd never seen so many colorful doors. I didn't know it then but this trip became the beginning of my obsession with colorful doors and discovering what might lay beyond.

A block or so later I could hear music. No one else did. Another block down the road, I stopped to listen more carefully. Yes, I heard music. Could it be bagpipes? We were following signs to the Edinburgh Castle because The Doric Tavern wasn't far from it. Plus, I wanted to see the castle before it got dark. However, being that far north, we learned it didn't get dark that time of year until around eleven o'clock. The music grew louder the closer we got and the bagpipes sounded stronger and clearer.

As we rounded the corner straight ahead there stood a single piper on a little berm. Twice now in the same day tears streamed uncontrollably down my cheeks. I began to seriously wonder what might be happening to my emotions. Being that close to a real piper with me actually standing at the foot of Edinburgh Castle felt a bit overwhelming. It seemed the Scottish piper serenaded just me.

To my novice's eye, the piper appeared dressed in authentic garb from head to toe. He wore a black cloth cap with a jiggling red pompom attached on the top, and a gold-crested brooch around on the left side. His reddish-brown hair seemed mostly covered by the cap. His auburn eyebrows and mustache weren't as remarkable as much as his hypnotizing blue eyes. I felt mesmerized as he moved his fingers ever so lightly creating such heart-tugging, haunting, soulful music. He wore a white shirt with the sleeves rolled up above his elbows and a teal blue tie with miniature orange crests like polka dots. His shirt was tucked into a kilt of large teal and orange plaid.

Comparing it against my Scottish Tartan cheat-sheet, he appeared to be from the Clan MacLennan. The teal might be more of a steely blue matching his eyes; it was hard to distinguish in the changing light. His black belt had a silver buckle about three inches square. I could barely see his knees as they were hidden except when he moved. Dangling in front of him hung a smallish cloth bag with three white tassels on a chain. His knee-high socks were of heavy white yarn and had a tassel hanging on the outside of each leg. His shoes were totally flat with no soles, maybe a soft leather, and the laces wound upwards in three loops to slightly above his ankle. It must have taken him hours to get dressed.

His rosy checks were puffed out as he blew hard into the shortest of the four pipes attached to the top of a black bag. He squeezed the black bag firmly with his left arm while the other arm extended down with his fingers on the top part of a pipe. His ten fingers were moving up and down along the black pipe. The ebony pipes, with scarlet and golden adornment, were connected at the top with gray cording, linking or maybe tying the pipes together. And he made phenomenal music, to me anyway. He played *Amazing Grace*, my mother's favorite song. I thought this might be a little prequel to Heaven. I could have stood there for hours listening but my companions were almost faint from hunger by now and not nearly as spellbound as I felt.

In Old Town we easily located the 17th century Doric Tavern, sort of a combination of Scottish, European, British pub-look, complete with brimming baskets overflowing with trailing flowers. We were greatly anticipating our first tastes of Scotland. The rustic dark floors with swag curtains seemed traditional décor but not outdated. The Victorian-style downstairs pub was cozy and we were seated upstairs in the dining room.

Ravenous, we began our feast with starters, sometimes called nibbles, our "appetizers" at home. We each ordered different nibbles so we could all have a taste. We sampled a homemade Cullen skink, a Scottish classic soup of smoked haddock, potatoes, onions and cream with warm bread and bright yellow butter. We tasted fresh local mussels steamed in a garlic, white wine and cream sauce. The final starter was homemade pasta filled with wild mushrooms and served in a cream sauce. We passed on the haggis bon bons. We just couldn't bring ourselves to try the haggis balls rolled in oatmeal, deep fried in creamed turnip sauce. Mark had venison; Martha had the crispy duck breast; Nina had rack of lamb. I selected salmon fillet with apple potatoes, and mango and lemon salsa with cherry tomatoes fresh off the vine. Every bite tasted like an explosion of flavors for my taste buds.

For dessert, I had their famous Sticky Toffee Pudding, a delectable delight with finger-licking butterscotch sauce and fresh cream. I'd had it once before in England and ever since then I searched menus for the heavenly dessert longing for another bite or seven. It's a steamed dessert consisting of moist sponge cake made with chopped dates, covered in a toffee sauce and often served with a vanilla custard or vanilla ice cream. I preferred the custard and Mark always preferred the ice cream. I shared one small bite per person, a generous sacrifice for sure. We shared and devoured Malt Whisky Truffles, served with orange coulis and a generous scoop of vanilla ice cream. Mark reported the scoop of vanilla ice cream to be exceptionally creamy and flavorful. He would know as he is a vanilla ice cream connoisseur. We had a drink of their homemade cider which tasted stout and not too sweet. It was a terrific beginning to tasting our way through Scotland for the upcoming week and an excellent way to end our first day in bonnie Scotland. Overfed and too tired to walk back the three miles, we hailed a black, four-door boxy taxi that returned us to our home-away-from-home.

Staying at a bed-and-breakfast meant breakfast would be included. Our day began with a hearty traditional "Full Scottish" meal that definitely was photo worthy. We sat at a corner table by the lacy curtained window as a young woman came by wearing a lovely embroidered sweater that I complimented her on. She said thank you and politely corrected me calling it a "jumper."

She explained what food eventually would be served. But first we were shown the sideboard (which I learned meant men's sideburns) lined with cold starters of assorted juices, plain yogurt with muesli sprinkled on top, and whole or sliced fruit. I spotted perfectly round, one-inch thick oatcakes with choices of raspberry jam (our jelly) or orange marmalade. There was a selection of cereals including Weetabix, which looked like granola bars but is really shredded wheat. I took just one square and bit into what tasted like a bale of hay. Next appeared a thick, tan-colored hot cereal called porridge and since I wasn't a fan of Cream of Wheat or oatmeal, I passed. The muffins were called buns and the buns were called baps.

We sat down with our assorted starters as the hot food arrived. Toast came next, cut diagonally, then fitted into an efficient little silver rack to keep it crisp but not hot or even warm. The toast, really browned bread, had been toasted but the British don't adhere to the American custom of toast being warm to melt the butter. They slather the butter onto the cold toast and then add a thin layer of something else, either sweet or savory. The enormous block of sunshine yellow butter sat on a china plate looking like it had just been delivered from the local dairy, not perfectly formed into a pint-size brick like at home. Thick marmalade came in a petite matching china bowl, and some locally made honey came in a jar. One lick of honey tasted like it had been flavored with sweet wildflowers or a sprig of whatever heather might taste like. Scottish honey is different from our clear, amber-colored honey in a plastic bear. The Scottish version is thicker and less sticky.

Even with the yogurt, juices, tea or coffee, cereals and toast, our host, grinning from ear-to-ear, brought out two oval platters. Presented impressively in sections were four items, one for each of us, whether we wanted it or not. In the first quadrant on the first platter were four half tomatoes, broiled and topped with a little cheese. Next came a rasher, or bacon, which is more like thinly sliced Canadian bacon, two slices each. Then came a scone-shaped tattie (really potato), sort of like our hash browns, and last for this platter were bangers, a fatter, thick version of our link sausage. Vegetables and protein were a great way to start the day and cholesterol wasn't an allowable topic on this trip.

Platter number two displayed sautéed mushrooms, baked beans (just like right out of the can), and one egg that they asked ahead of time how we'd like prepared. So on this plate came a mix of scrambled (for me), an over easy, a hard and a poached. Then came something that appeared to be dark chocolate or blackish sliced round cake. In fact, it is called "blood pudding." But it wasn't like any dark chocolate pudding I'd seen and was hoping for, even though only at nine o'clock, it's never too early for chocolate.

Pompously, I had vowed prior to this trip to try new foods and beverages. We promised ourselves we'd never darken the door of an American fast food restaurant on any foreign adventure except to purchase a soda when having to become a customer to use a restroom. But I didn't even take a nibble of blood pudding when informed the ingredients were pig's blood, fat, oats, barley and spices, all crammed in a length of intestine. I didn't want to be rude, so politely declined, rationalizing it had been such a huge meal I had all the fuel needed to start our first full day in Scotland. I wasn't the only one who passed on the blood pudding.

Stuffed, we decided it would be best to walk it off by strolling into the city. Upon arrival, we did what we traditionally do the first time in a new city: we rode the green and yellow, Guide Friday, Hop on/Hop off, double-decker bus for a city tour. We always sit on the top deck for prime viewing.

The tour bus drove by Scott Monument, a spire-like Victorian memorial in honor of the writer, Sir Walter Scott, with two hundred eighty-seven steps to the top, which we didn't climb although the view, I felt sure, would be remarkable. We saw the grand Balmoral Hotel, rode down Lothian Road, by St. John's Church, and the luxurious Caledonian Hotel seemingly made of milk chocolate-looking stone and columns surrounding the front entrance flanked by Scottish and English flags.

The tour took us by the Grassmarket and onto Victoria Street, the Lawnmarket, Gladstone's Land and High Kirk of St. Giles. On Chamber Street stood the National Museum of Scotland, which reminded me of Roman architecture with the clean tall columns of white granite; Greyfriars Bobby, a well-known pub with its famous landmark statue of a Skye Terrier named Bobby perched on a pedestal; John Knox House, up the Royal Mile and Edinburgh Castle that we would later tour. This castle was where Scottish monarchs were born in 1566. Next we saw Holyrood Palace, which was the home of Mary Queen of Scots. Contrary to what many think, it is not the official residence in Edinburgh of Queen Elizabeth.

Farther down the road we saw the Scottish Parliament building, a couple of universities, Queen's Park, Arthur's Seat, Regent Road, Burns Monument, Dugald Stewart monument on Calton Hill, who the guide said had been a popular philosopher and mathematician, Hanover Street, the modern city center, Market Street and ended at the Waverley Railway Station. To me it appeared that all of the monuments and buildings looked somewhat dark, maybe even dirty. When I asked the red-headed tour guide about it she replied that due to pollution, air and general old age, they are unable to clean the buildings by power washing because they would crumble. The process has to be done slowly by hand. Low-lying gray clouds might have added to the overall dreariness.

After the complete circle tour, we stayed on a while longer until we hopped off and toured museums, shops in Grassmarket, and spent the rest of the day moseying around this historic city. We walked on dreamy-sounding Candlemaker Row to Greyfriars Bobby. We rubbed his shiny nose for good luck; it was the only thing shiny on him. The plaque read that he was born in 1855 or 56 and died 14 January 1872. The story goes that Bobby became well-known and loved as he supposedly spent fourteen years guarding the grave of his owner until he died at age sixteen. As a dog lover, I totally believed this could happen.

At a stone church, the sharply arched entrance to the office seemed different than the more common softly rounded doorways. It was an over-size, well-worn, two-panel cherry red wooden door. In the middle of the left door hung a baroque-style black iron handle and matching curved hinges. It was well worth a photograph. I had already taken dozens of photos, trying to limit myself to fifty a day, but it wasn't happening this day. Each roll of film would be turned in and photos returned to me on printed paper to save in my photo albums to remind myself of memories and favorite sights years later. Most trips had resulted in multiple albums.

While strolling around, I peered down a narrow alley with two buildings so close one of the new dinky, compact Smart Cars couldn't have driven down. At the end of the alley stood a narrow five-story apartment building with the doors facing me. The doors were perfectly aligned one right on top of the other with the first floor door tan in color, second floor door charcoal, third floor blue door, fourth floor red door, and the top floor door a medium pink. As I pointed it out to my compatriots, Martha commented I might be infatuated with colorful doors. I admitted I thought so.

Old Town overflowed with sights and sounds. The two hundred-foot towering gothic Scott Monument made of sandstone honors Scottish author, Sir Walter Scott. Conveniently for us, it had a series of viewing platforms that we reached by narrow spiral staircases, giving a panoramic view of the city and surroundings. The highest platform was worth the two hundred eighty-seven steps. Catching our breath after the climb, our plaque reader, Nina, read the placard describing the memorial. There were sixty-eight figurative statues on the monument of which sixty-four were visible from the ground. In total, ninety-three persons were shown, plus a pig and two dogs.

We walked around Princes Street Gardens popping with colors of red and yellow begonias, manicured circles of greenery, rose gardens, and at the Ross Fountain, we stared up at the castle. Made of cast iron, the Ross Fountain is intricate with sculptures including several females depicting science, art, poetry and industry, topped with a woman gripping a cornucopia.

We'd been by Edinburgh Castle a number of times and now we had the time to enter. Smiling castle guards were milling about. The castle is situated on Castle Rock, an extinct volcano which formed after it erupted over three hundred million years ago. Castle Rock had also been a military base and royal residence for centuries. The castle had been built during the 12th century and is made of stone. The tensions between England and Scotland monarchies nearly always centered on the castle. Whoever held it ruled over the city and country. It was often under siege. Three flags were flying over the vaulted stone entrance as we walked over the empty moat below.

Upon entering, we encountered a young Robin Hood and Maid Marian, a brother/sister duo dressed in period costumes. Marian wore a fresh mint empire dress with little puffy sleeves and black summer sandals. Robin Hood, with his blunt-edged staff, wore a black coat, belted at his waist, over his black and red plaid, knee-length knickers. At the neck of his cloak was a bright green scarf. They both had soft reddish-blond hair and Marian didn't wear head gear but Robin wore the typical Robin Hood hat. After asking their mother if I could take a photo of this darling duo, she said yes. Their mother seemed pleased that we noticed and admired her efforts in creating such authentic 13th century costumes. Both

Marian and Robin posed for a photo, grinning shyly, with Robin proudly showing off his sword.

Once inside, we saw the Crown Jewels of Scotland, in other words, a jewel-encrusted crown, an elaborate sword and a scepter. Each holds great historical significance. We could see all over the city with views towards The Firth of Forth and hills. It had been a great vantage point to protect the city, especially with cannons facing out each window.

The gray clouds lifted as we reached the top of the castle and a ray of sun, like a spotlight drawing attention to a car lot at night, lit up Dugald Stewart Monument on Calton Hill. The overall appearance of the city became brighter.

The castle cannon, called the One O'clock Gun, fired earlier at one o'clock when we were touring and was startlingly loud. Fired every day except Sunday, Good Friday and Christmas Day, it was established in 1861 as a time signal for ships in the harbor at Leith and the Firth of Forth, two miles away. The gun was removed and replaced by several newer generations of guns. It had been an eighteen-pound muzzle-loading cannon, which needed four men to lay, and was fired from the Half Moon Battery. This had been replaced in 1913 by a thirty-two-pound breech-loader and in May 1952 by this twenty-five-pound Howitzer. We learned a lot of gun facts in a short amount of time.

Strolling back to our B&B, I felt like I had been temporarily transported into a fairytale, as one stone cottage had a fuchsia-painted, papa bear-size front door for the baby bear residence. They had dozens of hanging flower baskets somehow suspended or floating from the front of the house. I saw a limestone one-story home with a front door painted vivid red and climbing red roses on either side. The windows were cloaked in lace curtains and window boxes overflowed with red geraniums. It looked warm and welcoming.

Another home had a red Dutch door, where the bottom could be closed and the top half opened. The top half had been left partially opened. This homeowner had pots of blue pansies to the right of the door and purple and yellow flowers on the left. We also had a Dutch door at our home that opened onto a patio in our backyard. I had been infatuated with these doors since watching *Petticoat Junction* on television as a child and now had one of my own. There were other colorful doors but there was something about the red doors that really popped out. On our return walk, we saw dozens of doors painted in navy, slate blue, aqua, deep green, sunshine yellow, lime, sapphire, pea green, orange, teal, jade, periwinkle and ebony—a kaleidoscope— and not a white door in sight. I wondered who lived behind those colorful doors and why they chose those particular colors. I learned that a red door originally was painted to show that the owners had paid off their mortgage. Now it means "Welcome" so it made perfect sense why so many were that color. I became smitten, probably addicted, to colorful doors. I greatly exceeded my allotment of photos for the day.

The next morning, MapQuest instructions showed we had about one hundred miles to drive to our next destination, Edzell. We politely declined the full

Scottish breakfast and opted for pastries and fruit. We bid a fond farewell to Edinburgh and proceeded out of the city anticipating the next part of our journey. Martha, with her roundabout instruction sheet prepared for the day, got us through the first one just fine and at the next one turned onto Great Stuart Street that went onto the A90 on the Forth Road Bridge. We were on the M90 where we followed the River Tay a bit before turning east onto to the A90.

At Perth, we saw signs for St. Andrews but didn't take time to detour even though we knew it to be a famous landmark for those interested in golf. We weren't. We drove through scenic, wee towns and when we saw Brechin, the A90 turned due north and we knew we were within eight miles of Edzell. Every acre seemed to be farmland and crops. We spotted a pair of golden eagles soaring over countryside that looked like the hand of a great artist had dipped it in a palette of emerald and russet with some splotches of crimson and amethyst. On one side of the road stood a forest and the other farmland. Just past a golf course we left the roadway onto a smaller country carriageway. A little brownish round creature ambled across the road which sort of reminded me of the roadkill I'd spotted earlier. Then there were two, then several more. They were hedgehogs, all over the place fortunately not just flattened on the road. We drove out of farmland into Whishop Burn, a dense wall of timber with mixed aspen and birch trees. As we exited the forest we approached a stone arch that covered the one-lane road. Stopping before driving through the arch, I could see a sandstone building with a clock tower overshadowing the rest of the

33

picturesque structure. I took a picture. We were at the Edzell Arch, really the Dalhousie Arch. Late that afternoon we entered the village of Edzell, population six hundred. And I knew one of the six hundred and soon would know three more. We were going to visit and stay with a friend from Oregon who'd some years earlier married a Scottish man that included in the package deal his two children and a border collie, reportedly one of the smartest dogs on the planet. Her husband's name was Andy, not Jamie the hero in a Scottish book series I had been devouring called *Outlander*.

Once again I shared my pre-trip knowledge with my trio. This little village wasn't as old as it looked. Built around 1840, many buildings were relatively new even though the Edzell Castle is much older. During World War II the town served as a Royal Air Force airfield located east of town. In the 1960s, the airfield became a U.S. Naval base.

The main attraction was Edzell Castle which sadly had crumbled mostly into ruins. The original structure was built by the Abbott family around 1100. The property passed to the Stirlings of Glenesk by marriage to the Lindsays in 1358. It stayed with the Lindsays until 1715 and they built the castle to what it had been in the good times. By 1757, debt increased so much that the Lindsays were forced to sell. Edzell Castle later passed to the Dalhousie family, who retained ownership for some time. In 1923, the walled garden passed into state care and they sold the rest of the castle in 1935. Edzell Castle and gardens are cared for by Historic Scotland, a

Deleen Wills

society that oversees and cares for historical and archaeological sites. Another history lesson over.

We pulled up in front of the two-story Glenesk Cottage on Dunlappie Road, easy to find just off to the left as we exited the Arch. The house had been constructed of tan bricks with big wooden windows trimmed with boxes of flowers, and a large reddish door. Their black and white border collie greeted us with his entire body wagging. We were introduced to Dillon, their four-legged family member, who'd be our companion during our stay.

With introductions for the first-timers and hugs from me, we settled into our temporary home. We met dad Andy, son Joe and daughter Maryann. Mark and I were taking over Maryann's bedroom which turned out also to be Dillon's room. We loved dogs and our golden retriever, Jasper, stayed at home with our trusted doggie sitter, Nita. Dillon caused me to feel a little homesick; therefore, he got to sleep with us. But really, we were sleeping in his bed just minus Maryann.

Joyce made a delicious meal and we all got acquainted. Looking out the kitchen window I could see their backyard with freshly cut green grass, summer flowers and trees, wide open sky filled with puffy white clouds with distinct flat bottoms, rolling hills and farmland, and what was left of Edzell Castle. During dinner, Joe filled Andy and Joyce in on his day at school. Even though they were speaking English, it could have been Gaelic to us. I glanced at Joyce with furrowed brow and she laughed and told

35

Andy and Joe to slow down so we could understand them. It didn't help much.

Around ten o'clock, and still with plenty of daylight, we strolled about twenty minutes to Edzell Castle. Tall purple and white flowers reminded me of our purple lupine at home. Dairy cows sauntered to the fence to meet us and a couple of horses expected the carrots Joyce loaded us with.

A seven hundred-year-old beech tree at the entrance seemed to welcome us with open arms to the sandstone Edzell Castle. Even though long after the official closing time for the day, Joyce knew a way in. We scrambled over the gate and we were in. For being a ruin, the large fireplace still looked impressive. By entering illegally, I felt sort of clandestine milling around and exploring the remains of what once had been a remarkable castle. I took photos through windows and arched vacant doorways. There were niches for birds to nest and dainty purple and white flowers growing from the walls with the sun and stars etched in the bricks above.

The gardens were immaculate with a three-foot stone fence as the boundary, triangular-shaped raised beds, rounded boxwoods, and perfect square plots of scarlet flowers. Joyce informed us that the British use the term "garden" when flowers and vegetables are grown. A "yard" is just grass. There were sculptures and planets carved into wooden panels. Several healthy red squirrels were bounding around seeming not to care we'd broken the law and entered their domain after hours. In the garden wall, various plaques were still in place including a Coat of Arms of Sir David Lindsay. Resident peacocks were noisy and disrespectfully dropping grayish-brown, smelly deposits along the Lindsay burial aisle. Even though in ruins, the site still was much more well-preserved than I had imagined from my readings.

Ambling back, we spotted a neighbor's garden that could have been in "Better Homes and Gardens" magazine. It appeared picture-perfect with mani-cured boxwoods, every size and height of colorful flowers, flawlessly shaped bushes and, way in the back, a wee stone cottage at the end of the pebble lane. I wanted to live there.

Roses were plentiful and Joyce pointed out soft yellow Sow Thistle, pale peach Cranesbill, pastel blue Harebell, lavender Dog-violet, white Convol-vulus, buttery Celandine and hot pink Anemone—a bouquet anyone would enjoy.

Early the next morning while everyone else was either still sleeping or drinking coffee, I went for a walk. This became a habit that I started on earlier trips, getting out before other tourists, and was certainly no problem in this wee burgh. Homes around the neighborhood were different from each other, nothing cookie cutter here. One homeowner had painted the stone all white complete with a light blue door and the same color blue on the window shutters. Another house, constructed of multicolored stones, had a deep purple front door adorned with a floral wreath. Down the avenue I found The Tuck Inn, bright red and conjoined like a Siamese twin to The Pharmacy, a bright lime green. Not far away stood the Inglis Memorial Hall with the clock tower that we glimpsed coming through the arch the day before. The Hall seemed distinguished and maybe even proud to show me its ornate stained-glass windows and I noticed that the downspouts even had striking touches as if they had been hand carved.

At dinner the previous night, Joyce had told us the history. Around 1860, Mr. Inglis had been a well-liked minister of the parish. He and his wife had thirteen children, many of whom went on to do great things, like one son who became chairman of the London stock exchange. He was later knighted. He presented Edzell with the Hall in memory of his parents and an uncle, a resident farmer in Glen Esk who shared his medical knowledge throughout the area free of charge. The Hall housed two halls, a library with a reading room, parish council room, caretaker's flat and various other rooms, all furnished at the son's expense. In commemoration of Queen Victoria's Jubilee, he also gifted over five thousand books which he selected and had specially bound so that they would survive much handling.

Joyce worked on the military base as a teacher. We drove to the base to see her classroom and do a little shopping at the commissary. I glanced through the souvenir area and spotted a miniature sculpture of the Edzell Arch in the exact same golden color, flanked by bushes on both sides, front and back. The depiction appeared architecturally accurate and intricate, and would be a precious remembrance. Joyce told me that the creator was a well-known man named Ian MacGregor Fraser, and Fraser Creations were extremely collectible. My first souvenir from Edzell. And fortunately for me, right next to the Arch sat a mini-Edinburgh Castle. Knowing we'd not be returning that way, I snapped up another Fraser collectible. She mentioned there had been speculation and rumors the base would be closing soon. Her premonition turned out to be correct as it closed the following year.

The Scottish Highlands

Our hostess-with-the-mostest thought her stateside friends should see some of her adopted country, so she orchestrated a two-day road trip and she would be our driver. Early the next morning the five of us climbed into her Volvo and drove to Pitlochry, a fair-size town seeming to have been plopped down at the base of its own mountain, Ben-Y-Vrackie. With the crisp, clean air, friendly people, stunning scenery and superior shopping for handmade Scottish wares where we helped support the local economy, it was a memorable place for sure. There is a dam on the River Tummel with a fish ladder for the salmon run. The dam created Loch Faskally and was a picturesque spot to start our discovery of the Highlands and lochs.

We stopped at the Caithness glass factory next. What makes their glass so extraordinary is that they take the inspiration from the colors of the landscape—heather purple, warm earth tones and the blue of the lochs. They developed original techniques for abstract designs, as well as using conventional processes. Each piece is entirely unique and Caithness Glass is regarded as one of the world's most respected producers of museum-quality paperweights. I had to have one.

They provided a small flyer about the heritage of heather which read, "Heather's use as bedding is a link between its domestic and its herbal or medicinal role. The old herbalists knew that 'they who lie down at night faint and weary' on a heather bed, 'rise in the morning active and lively' because of its restorative properties." There are actually two types of heather, the common one called Calluna, and Erica, sometimes called "bell heather." Then there are two species of Erica, the bell heather and cross-leaved heath. The cross-leaved heath has all of its flowers at the top of the stem. We had purple heather in our backyard at home. It was the common variety, I learned after being educated on heather varieties but it was my personal tribute to Scotland, my motherland.

While carefully scrutinizing each choice, I felt drawn to the ones with blues, like the water. I found just the one—an orb perfectly round with a ribbon of blue intertwined with a separate ribbon of pink, almost the color of the wild fuchsia hedgerows we'd been seeing. The ribbons started together at the bottom, swirled up and around the globe until the ribbon got smaller towards the top and disappeared into the clearness. There were dozens and dozens of dots that seem uniform when looking straight on but when picking it up and gazing through it, look like millions of stars, light-years away. And this keepsake went home with me where it still graces our home and is a cherished memento of my first journey to Scotland.

Before getting back into the car, I glanced down at a thistle, the Scottish national flower. It felt prickly to touch and most knew better. The outer part of this thistle showed off its layers of pointy green petals. The three top levels were bright purple in the center with lighter lavender tips. It reminded me of fireworks on the Fourth of July. It was a thistle in its infancy and nearby was one fully bloomed and wholly bright purple.

Not far down the road we came upon a modern-looking white castle, called Blair Castle. But it wasn't modern at all since it had been built in 1269 and was the home to Dukes of Atholl Clan Murray. Upon entering we traversed a narrow hallway I dubbed the "corridor of horns" because the entire hallway appeared lined with skulls and antlers from deer, elk and other critters. In the sitting area stood an enormous cabinet full of Atholl custom-made china plates. In the dining room a table had been laid out and looked ready to host fourteen guests complete with one large elk statue balanced carefully on a silver base sitting smack dab in the middle of the table. A guest would have been eyeball to eyeball with the stag. Expansive landscape paintings flanked a mammoth fireplace.

Another room showcased stunning gowns from first ladies of Atholl and it appeared easy to tell the era in which they were worn. On the way out, we stopped by the souvenir shop and lo and behold, there sat a wee white Blair Castle perfectly shrunk down and made into a Fraser Creation. Another sculpture added to my collection.

Even though we were in the Scottish Highlands, we weren't too far from water as seagulls noisily greeted us. These were much more striking than those on the Oregon coast with solid black heads and a matching black shawl down their necks with all white bodies. I wondered if all birds and sheep had black faces in bonnie Scotland.

Once again we were serenaded by a piper, this one dressed appropriately in the Clan Murray tartan of grays and oranges with a deep crimson bag on the pipes. It took me to a different plane, a different space, a different time. I didn't recognize the song but it didn't matter; it was another piper on bagpipes. My companions just didn't seem to grasp the deep tugging, haunting sound of bagpipes had on me and stirred my soul, every fiber to my core. Obviously, they had no ancestral Scottish blood coursing through their veins. They just didn't get it...at all. I chose to disregard the occasional eye-rolling and sighing.

The Highlands is a historic area of Scotland and the term is used to describe the area north and west of the Highland Boundary Fault. It's best just to look at a map to see the division between the Lowlands and the Highlands.

The Highlands and lochs seemed to have loftier slopes and valleys, with borders of stone and thousands of blackface sheep along the roadside. Joyce was a wealth of information and pronunciation assistance. First, we were never to say "lock" for "loch." Lock is something they put a key in. She had us try the word breathing through the back of our mouth (or called pus in Scotland), "lawccchhh." It was definitely an air and breathing thing. Same thing goes for Bach; it's not a "k." I suggest before anyone goes to Scotland, pull up YouTube for a quick tutorial on correct pronunciations.

A whiteface sheep would have been out of the norm and we probably would have stopped to take its picture as a novelty. The blackface sheep were hearty and wooly and the lambs gave the appearance of little fluff balls just waiting to be petted. We rarely saw a meadow or hillside without dozens. We pulled over to the side of the road for yet another photo op. A friendly elderly Scottish couple out for a stroll stopped by to greet us. We were parked on their property. We had a lovely conversation but I under-stood little because of their brogue. Joyce translated their niceties when we got back in the car.

The area looked sparsely populated with more peaks in the distance. The vegetation changed and Joyce pointed out Scots pine, the only area to have these trees. She showed us vivid yellow shrubs she called Broom. I reminded her we have Scotch Broom covering the valley where we reside in Oregon. Even though vibrant and pretty, it causes great angst to those with allergies in early spring and had been gobbling up hillsides in our area. Although showy and colorful, it is considered an invasive species.

And then there was Nessie of Loch Ness. It's a vast, deep blue lake with fishing and sightseeing boats and a castle, and is situated at the base of rolling hills. At the visitor's information center, we saw Nessie up close and personal. I even stood next to her and had a photo taken. We didn't see her in the water even though we stared, or rather gazed, as nonchalantly as possible while we drove the entire way around the loch on our way to Urquhart Castle.

But we did see plenty of large, healthy osprey diving for their lunch, sometimes successful, sometimes not. I had my camera at the ready. I freely admit we were searching for Nessie. As we drove around the loch, purple heather had just started blooming in the Highlands.

Urquhart Castle sits beside Loch Ness and dates from the 13th century. The brochure explained it played a role in the Wars of Scottish Independence in the 14th century. It had been raided on several occasions by the MacDonald Earls of Ross. The castle was granted to the Clan Grant in the early 1500s as fighting with the MacDonalds continued. It had been partially destroyed in the late 1600s and continued to decay until it was placed in state care in the 20th century. I could see why it had become one of the most visited castles in Scotland with the spectacular view overlooking Loch Ness. Walking across the waterless moat on a wooden bridge, we were able to amble and climb to the top. I took too many pictures of the loch through arches and glass-less windows. I heard music from across the loch but no one else did. Clearly they weren't as tuned in to bagpipes as I had become; I had a sixth sense for the pipes. I wondered how many visiting sleepwalkers in the past hundreds of years had innocently plunged to their deaths in the loch below from the sheer drop-off. From the vast, stunning loch we drove to the city of Inverness, population about thirty-five thousand, located on the River Ness complete with its own castle appropriately named Inverness Castle. Inverness means "Mouth of the River Ness" and is regarded as the capital of the Highlands. It lies close to two important battle sites but the one I recognized was the Battle of Culloden, which took place on the Culloden Moor.

Joyce had made overnight accommodations for us at Ardmuir House, right along the bank of the river. Our room looked sparsely but pleasantly furnished with a wooden chair, a nightstand, sink and double bed with a distinct groove up the middle. We would share a bathroom and toilet down the hallway. The floral rose-patterned wallpaper matched the bedspread and curtains, towels and pink carpet. Out our window we saw a brick church on the bank along with a sprawling low bridge that crossed the wide Ness River.

While walking to dinner we saw a mother pushing a wee bairn (meaning little child) in a pram (stroller). Thanks again to our interpreter, we learned many Scottish and British words. Walking back to Ardmuir House after a delicious meal we heard music and stumbled upon a Ceilidh. Joyce pronounced it "kay-lee" and explained it involves Gaelic folk music and dancing. She said we had to have a wee peek. We did and went in, thoroughly enjoying people of all ages singing, playing instruments and dancing Scottish jigs, another dance called "The Frisky," and to top it off, step dancing. I vowed to take step dancing lessons when we returned home.

In my research before our trip, I read up on historical happenings in Scotland and this next site we were touring was a biggie. The Battle of Culloden had also been highlighted in the *Outlander* historical fiction/nonfiction book series. I had just finished reading book three, the one specifically where the battle happened. Claire, an ex-combat nurse, had been visiting the Scottish Highlands with her 1940s husband Frank. Claire is out walking by herself and comes across a circle of standing stones, which are fairly common all over Britain. She walks through a cleft stone in the circle and disappears. She reappears in 1743, where her life takes a big turn. Because one of her passions (along with new Scottish husband, Jamie Fraser) is history, Claire knows what will happen. She knew that on April 16, 1746, on Drumossie Moor overlooking Inverness, a well-supplied Hanoverian army led by the Duke of Cumberland, also the son of King George II, annihilated the much smaller army of Lord John Murray, and the leader he mistrusted, Prince Charlie. This had been the bloodiest of all the Jacobite battles. Prince Charlie's choice of rough, marshy ground was catastrophic, and the Jacobite swords and daggers were no match for the Hanoverian cannon and guns. More than a thousand Jacobites were killed and around three hundred Hanoverians died. The battle was over in an hour. But she was stuck in her present-day world and didn't know what she would return to find Jamie, dead or alive.

We walked the path of crushed stones out into the middle of the green battlefield thick with brush and weeds. A large stone memorial cairn was erected in 1881. Duncan Forbes assembled the headstones that mark the mass graves of fallen Jacobite soldiers. The battlefield is kept in similar condition to how it had been on April 16, 1746. We saw the twenty-foot tall memorial cairn. There are many engraved stones for clans: Fraser, McGillivray, MacLean, MacLauchlan, Athol Highlanders, Donald, Mackintosh, Cameron and Stewart of Appin. Another sign read, "The Battle of Culloden was fought on this moor 16th April 1746. The graves of the gallant highlanders who fought for Scotland & Prince Charlie are marked by the names of their clans." Once again I got teary but this wasn't the same reaction from tears hearing bagpipes or the first time entering my country. I felt a sadness deep to my very soul and sense of gloom in this area; it wasn't pleasant at all. I felt relieved to leave this awful place.

In *Outlander*, the fictitious character and hero, Jamie Fraser, and some clansman survived. Jamie, to those who have read this book series, was sort of a secret "code word" for many American women when the books came out. Joyce had been the one who introduced me to the historical, time-warping series. There were printed cartoons and jokes that expressed my feelings well, such as: "Relax honey, I'm not leaving you for Jamie Fraser. He's a fictional character from a book. Believe me, if he were real, I'd be long gone by now." "My search for a Jamie Fraser may be getting out of control. Saw a cute red-haired guy at the grocery store today, asked if he could act Scottish. They made me leave." "Yes, dear, I did replace all your pants with kilts and I won't apologize for it."

Now, looping back towards Edzell we stopped at another ruin, Dunnottar Castle, perched on a bluff overlooking the North Sea. As we rounded a corner, there sat a red telephone booth on a green patch of grass while one black and two white goats were milling close by chomping on the lush grass. On a grassy knoll stood a piper. The haunting melody drifted away in the breeze. I wondered if someone down the coastline would hear him and be perplexed, questioning where the music had come from. Would they think they were hearing things like I had?

Dunnottar ruins looked different from other castles. It has a vantage point on the northeast coast and castles were built in strategic locations and for defensive purposes. This castle became best known as the place where the Honours of Scotland, or the crown jewels, were hidden from Oliver Cromwell's invading army in the 17th century. The chapel is said to have been founded in the 5th century. At each castle we visited, I wondered who chiseled and carved the thousands of stones it took to make the castles.

Purple heather, thistles and white weeds covered the ground. We climbed all over the castle, peeking through windows, taking photos through arches towards fields of unusually pretty weeds and down to the sea. On the ledge stood an aggressive seagull and we found out quickly she was protecting her speckled young ones in a nest. They were camou-flaged, matching the stonework and hard to spot.

Looking down the coastline, a bird caught my eye that I knew wasn't the typical seagull. Several landed on the cliffs below. I whipped out my binoculars to get a closer look and spied orange and black around their deep inset eyes plopped on the top part of white cheeks. I pulled out my Birds of Scotland tri-fold guide to see what I could find out about these orange-billed, squatty creatures. Was there such a creature called a sea parrot? Was it a lost exotic penguin looking like it was dressed for a prom in a tuxedo? Not with those orange feet and beaks. A few more flew in bending their wings like they were double-jointed. Balancing on the edge of the steep grassy and rocky cliffs looked dangerous and they flopped their wings to keep balance in the breeze. They acted and looked like silly clowns. My guidebook revealed they were puffins. And there were a few dozen that seemed off the beaten path as other colonies were up and down the coastline but not really in this area. I learned that baby puffins are called pufflings; how cute is that?! I learned a bit of puffin-speak and that they mate for life, live most of their lives at sea, resting on the waves when not swimming. They feast on little fish like herring or sardines and are on land several months to have their pufflings. They can live twenty years or more and live in a colony. I liked what I read but didn't have time to delve into their lifestyle much more than a fleeting glance. I always enjoyed birds and nature and vowed to search them out again in the future.

I could see where land jutted out into the sea and curved back inland. There were dozens of different colors of green in the grasses, trees, bushes and shrubbery. Exploring this castle with its views and vistas seemed a different experience than the other castles, maybe because it stood on a peninsula surrounded by steep cliffs that drop one hundred sixty feet below to the North Sea. We walked down to the sea not bothering the uncaring sheep grazing near the pathway. This wasn't a typical sandy beach but was littered with rough black rocks. I pocketed two interestingly shaped ones to take home for our rock garden.

Leaving the castle and heading back to Edzell, the hills flattened out and the roads were lined with random posts with thin wire stretched from one fence post to the next that barely would contain any animal. I saw some cows up ahead but they were different than the brown and white dairy cows that were typical. Joyce pulled over and we hopped out to see our first Highland "coos," extremely hairy cows, but pronounced "coo-ooz." They were brindle with long wavy hair from the top of the back hanging down below their bellies and over their eyes. I couldn't tell if she was looking at me or not. Nor could I tell if one was ready to charge at me with the two long horns or if they were docile pets. A small calf didn't care we were there, instead intently ate lunch, with momma's hair so long the baby's head appeared lost underneath her.

The landscape looked intriguingly colorful and the clouds with the sun peeking through frequently changed it all. I stood mesmerized gazing at the clouds changing shapes as they passed quickly by. In the distance, dark virga almost reached the ground as I could see a rain shower.

Sometimes the roadway narrowed, usually not much wider than one car width with no shoulders, nor were there lines painted in the middle or sides. Since there weren't signs indicating a suggested speed limit, our driver seemed to zoom through the countryside faster than I would but she knew the roads; we didn't.

That evening we piled into two cars and drove about forty-five minutes to the historic Drovers Inn, a white building covered in vines and flowers with a big wooden front door. It sat in the middle of an intersection with a nearby village called Memus. I heard quiet bagpipes indicating they were some distance away. Joyce said it was fairly commonplace and she'd forgotten how unique it really was to her adopted country. We never figured out why I could hear the pipers before anyone else and sometimes heard them when no one else did. I figured it was the sixth sense for bagpipes I had been gifted with. No one else thought so.

First glance inside The Drovers Inn revealed its welcoming wooden bar. They were known for using local foods and, whenever possible, from farms they knew and trusted. Inset in one wall of the restaurant was a wood-burning stove fireplace combo to warm up the winter nights. The tables and chairs were made of dark wood and the entire place looked shadowy yet cozy. The bar stretched out in the middle of the front room with dozens of scotch bottles proudly displayed. This was whisky country. Pictures adorned the walls depicting scenes and livestock from this area. It was named "The Drovers Inn" because men used to drive the cattle through the area and stop here for a pint and a meal. The two men in our group taste-tested eighteen, then twenty-five and finally thirty-year-old scotch, commenting the older it was the smoother it got. I took a sniff and it emotionally transported me into a lumber sawmill that some friends owned about thirty miles from my childhood home out in the country. But it also smelled like an orange vanilla soda, an odd combination, yet familiar and soothing.

Scrumptious aromas wafted from the kitchen. The Drovers Inn specialized in prawns and beef. Mark had a venison dish and I had the crisp prawns and spinach fritters with lemon crème fraîche and fries. Others had grilled sirloin steak and pan-fried fillet of sea bass with homemade mashed potatoes. Even though we were stuffed, several of us had to try the house specialty called Spotted Dick, a British pudding (any desserts are called pudding it seems) in a rounded shape made with suet, dried fruit and currants served with custard. We weren't disappointed. One doesn't forget certain experiences in their lives and this meal would be one for my books. Fine friends and ambiance had a lot to do with it.

As we waddled out from one of the best meals we'd ever had, against the fence were several friendly Highland coos, with horns poking through their long hair, eye-less but with visible brown noses. I knew they were watching us carefully. I fed one some grasses yet never saw her eyes. How can something be cute and a little scary?

We pulled out of the restaurant parking lot around ten o'clock and I could see the stars just popping out in the night sky. When we arrived home, we strolled to Edzell Castle one more time. I felt in a bit of denial knowing the next morning we were leaving to continue our trip seeing more of Scotland.

Hugs and thanks early the next morning brought tears to my eyes and as we drove out the Edzell Arch, I doubted I'd be this way again.

One decade later, we would meet new friends who moved from California and settled in our town.

Bob had retired from the Navy and when I asked where he served, he replied, "In Scotland but you've never heard of the place."

"Try me."

"A little town called Edzell."

"Really? Tell me about your time there then I'll share something with you," I laughed.

Almost There!

With about a three-hour drive ahead of us, we backtracked on the A90 until Perth, then dropped due south and at the A90 went onto the M90. Seeing signs for Edinburgh to the east and Glasgow to the west, we didn't deviate but carried on southbound. I praised Martha to the heavens for brilliantly navigating us through the labyrinth of roundabouts, and Mark for his expert driving abilities.

The countryside looked just as green and lush as where we'd come from but with more hillsides and plenty of sheep. We turned from the A70 back onto B7080 and at a junction turned south on B740 through Crawfordjohn, paralleling the Crawick Water, much like a stream, now meandering west before dropping south. At the B740 junction intersecting with A76 we turned back towards the east and the roadway became Glasgow Road, a rural single carriageway where the posted mileage sign stating 60 mph seemed way too fast.

At the dinky burgh of Kirkconnel, we were less than one mile away. Entering Sanquhar we stopped so I could take a photo of the sign that read

"Welcome to Sanquhar, Please Drive Carefully." The sign had been thrust solidly into the ground and was surrounded by a short stone fence. Inside the fence were hundreds of tiny bright yellow flowers that poked up through the uncut grass.

Finally. On July 10, a momentous day in my lifetime record book, we arrived at the hometown of my Scottish ancestors. I had been half expecting, or at the very least hoping for, a bagpipe serenade as it surprisingly often had happened. I knew I should have written ahead of time letting them know a prodigal daughter had returned, even generations later. As we drove down Glasgow Road it became High Street and we went right through the grounds of Lorimer Park. Off to the left I spotted Saint Bride's Parish Church sticking up above pointy-roof homes. We'd be searching for headstones in the church's cemetery later, specifically looking for my great-great grandmother, Jean Wightman Lorimer.

Our first stop was the Tolbooth Museum situated in the historic Tollbooth gaol, the old jail. For some reason, the Tolbooth Museum dropped the second "l" in the original spelling of the Tollbooth jail. The two-story building had two sets of stairs, one from the right and the other from the left, meeting at a landing that led to the entrance. A tall clock tower with a dome at the top had been previously used as both a tollbooth and a jail and skillfully converted into a museum. We watched an informative ten-minute film and dove back in time seeing the world-famous tradition of Sanquhar knitting, what life was like as a miner, and the history and customs. We time-traveled through three centuries of local literature, experiencing what everyday life had been like in Sanquhar for the earliest people. Mark, being the wonderful son-in-law that he is, recorded it on our video camera for my mother.

After viewing the film, artifacts, knitted gloves and pieces of history, we also discovered a bit about what it might have been like to be a prisoner in the Sanquhar jail as we gingerly crept down creaky stairs to a damp room with a dirt floor and thick stone walls on the ground floor. The shadowy, spooky room lit up when the sunbeam hit the floor like it had illegally snuck through a slit in the grimy wall. A shoeless, long-haired male mannequin held a tin plate with two biscuits and purple vegetables. An iron collar and a chain were attached to the wall by the side of the prison door. It was called a "joug" and held a prisoner by the neck. I felt calmer once we left this gloomy, somber, creepy place.

Outside in the sunshine, Nina put on her official narrator's cap and read the placard affixed to the wall. "Tolbooth. Built in 1731-35 to replace an earlier Tolbooth which was in a ruinous condition. The stone came from the newly vacant Sanquhar Castle. The architect was William Adam, from the family who went on to enjoy royal patronage as architects. This building was the administrative centre of the town, with the Provost and Baillies meeting upstairs. Tolls were collected, and public weights and measures were kept here by the Burgh Officer. The poet, Robert Burns, was admitted as an Honorary Burgess in 1794."

I was particularly interested in this old jail because my mother's favorite grandpa was a sheriff in Nebraska and my youngest brother worked in the sheriff's office in Linn County, Oregon. We also got directions to my family castle.

About three blocks south on High Street, our next stop was the historic two-story, three-bay house incorporating a rare bow-fronted shop window forming the post office. It is the oldest in the world, not only proudly displayed on a black oval plaque engraved in silver but the Guinness Book of World Records recognized it, too. It started out for mail carriages, with stables behind for horses to rest. As I stood there, I conjured up a vision of my great-great grandparents going in and out of this very post office, possibly writing to their relatives in the United States of America.

I'd never seen a display window at the post office before so read a printed sheet that announced itself as being a "Statement of Special Interest" explaining that bow-fronted shops began to develop in the mid 18th century along with more formal shop faces. They offered superior display space and more light and made a statement that the building was a shop of some form and open for business.

The two-story post office seemed scrunched between two taller buildings. There were two identical, well-worn burgundy doors separated only by a panel of white wall. This confounded me. Both doors seemed identical with a four-pane window on the top half. The four panes on the left door were covered with maps and flyers announcing upcoming town events. The door on the right had one vacant quadrant with the others filled with more announce-ments.

Looking more closely I found a handle on the left door and no handle on the right door. One was clearly an entrance and one the exit. To the right of the exit door was a brass mail slot built into the white wall. It didn't seem like that busy an establishment to warrant two doors. When pushing open the door on the left, I walked four steps to another burgundy door that led to the lobby where a cash register sat on top of one counter. The room appeared clean but seemed gloomy, being illuminated by one lightbulb dangling from a cord in the ceiling. With no one present, I made a quick right and exited out the proper door. We saw a sign on a building close by that read "Robert Burns Poet Slept Here August 25th 1787."

I knew my family's country had once been a separate kingdom with its capital being Edinburgh. When the coal and metals industries started, Scotland began improving financially by manufacturing iron, steel, fabrics, granite, papermaking and printing, plus shipbuilding and abundant fishing off the east coast and, of course, a world-renowned beverage—whisky. Farming and forestry were big despite large areas of countryside which were far from ideal for top-class agriculture.

Scotland has produced its share of legendary entertainers including writer and poet, Robert Burns, or Rabbie Burns to the Scottish, who I studied in high school. He wrote the poem which became the song "*Auld Lang Syne*," and many others that are well-known to the Scots. Then there is the dreamy Sean Connery, best known for portraying the character James Bond, starring in seven films between 1962 and 1983. I also knew that music bands Nazareth and

The Average White Band plus many more talented musical artists and lots of engineers and inventors too, hailed from Scotland—now my country, also.

My Castle

We hopped in the car and drove south about one mile from the center of town and found the castle sign. Traipsing up the unkempt grass path to the castle and being very careful not to step on clumps of Scottish bluebells, there before us was probably the worst looking ruins we'd seen the entire trip. Not much recognizable was left standing except a stone wall with an arched entrance and a disguisable outline of a stone house. It looked as though years-old weeds, bushes and moss were bonding together most of the structure. I carefully stepped over broken stones scattered on the ground and approached the doorway. There was no longer a door nor any relatives to swing it open to welcome a long-lost lassie from America with a big hug. But there I stood in the boyhood home where my great grandfather, Thomas O. Lorimer, was born in 1848 in one of these rooms. My sweet, demure grandmother was his daughter. She had smiling soft brown eyes, white hair soft to my touch and creamy, white, smooth skin with rosy cheeks never needing modern makeup. I never once witnessed the fiery temper that this nationality of people and her father were known for. I take after my grandmother with our pale complexion and fair-hair except my eyes are blue.

I felt paralyzed, unable to move from the entrance of my castle where the door once opened and closed. How many doors had been replaced over the centuries, I wondered. I closed my eyes and tried to imagine the castle door. I envisioned thick wood planks with a black iron handle. It would have been brown from the wood, not from paint. The stone arched doorway appeared surprisingly short, standing five feet six inches: there didn't seem to be a lot of head space above me. People overall were shorter and smaller in the 1200s even though I'd heard from family lore that William Wallace was a giant man. Mary, Queen of Scots, was close to six feet tall.

As I stood in the castle ruins perched on the rise, it felt a little eerie, like I was coming home, yet I'd never been there before. I didn't touch a thing, not a stone, not the wall, not the crumbled doorway. I had no desire to be like Claire in the *Outlander* book walking into the stone circle then travelling back hundreds of years to the primitive, violent time without running water and electricity. To even think about that evil captain Randall gave me shivers. Yet, pondering Jamie Fraser in a kilt was certainly tempting and fascinating, but not enough to be transported back to a past century.

I could faintly hear a lone piper and a chill ran down my spine. I couldn't see him but the sounds seemed to be coming from the center of town about a mile away. Maybe he was even farther away and the melodic tones floated along with the breeze. This turned out to be commonplace in Scotland but never taken lightly by me. I recognized the song *Scotland the Brave*, a patriotic song and the unofficial national anthem, *O Flower of Scotland* being the true national anthem. I had my share of Scottish CDs at home that

I'd been listening to for years, usually when my husband happened to be out of the house; let's just say he wasn't as enamored with bagpipes as I had become. I knew only the first stanza and chorus of this haunting song. I hummed along, but in my head I sang the words loudly and proudly:

"Hark, when the night is falling, Hear, hear the pipes are calling, Loudly and proudly calling down through the glen. There where the hills are sleeping, now feel the blood a leaping, high as the spirits of the old highland men.

Towering in gallant fame, Scotland my mountain home, High may your proud standards gloriously wave. Land o' the high endeavor, land o' the shining river, land o' my heart forever, Scotland the Brave." And I was weepy again which quickly became more like a river of tears.

I knew the history of my castle. I found from historical papers that the Crichton family came to Britain from Hungary and built the castle to be their family home situated on the southern approach to the former royal burgh of Sanquhar in Dumfries and Galloway. The castle became a stronghold bordered on the west by the River Nith, to the north by a small rise, and by a ditch running along the remainder of the boundary.

Chronicles show that William de Crichton was mentioned about 1240. Thomas de Crichton, his son, had been one of those barons who swore loyalty to Edward the First in 1296. Most think the castle was built in the mid-1200s but I couldn't find any exact date. He and his wife had three sons with decades of pedigrees and titles.

The end of the Crichton power was the result of an extravagant and wasteful party. In July 1617, the King of Great Britain travelled through Scotland to Glasgow on his way home and stopped at the castle. The Crichton family welcomed him with a show so huge that it bankrupted them. Royalty never paid for these parties hosted in homes of their true blue. I read that Lord Crichton escorted the king to bed carrying a lighted torch made from thirty thousand pound bond notes that the king owed Lord Crichton. By 1639, the family moved to Ayrshire and sold their holdings in Sanquhar to Sir Douglas, Earl of Queensberry who built the pink sandstone, Drumlanrig Castle, ten miles south of Sanquhar near Thornhill.

However, neither the Crichton clan nor Sir Douglas were my family. William Lorimer was. William III was the son of William Lorimer II and his wife, Elizabeth Wallace. He was my great-great-grandfather. As caretaker of the property, he lived in the castle as a full-time employee. William III married Jean Wightman, daughter of Alexander Wightman and his wife, Jean Bell.

William III and Jean resided in the castle where they had eight children, including my great grandfather Thomas, born in 1845. I could only imagine what a fine childhood to have an entire estate to roam freely. Sadly, Jean, my great-great-grandmother, died young at age 46 in 1852, leaving William with many young children. Great-great-grandpa William continued to work at the castle but finally left in 1872 with son Thomas for a new life in America.

My great grandfather, Thomas Oliver Lorimer, married Ann E. Proctor on February 23, 1877. He died June 3, 1926, twenty-eight years to the day before my birth and is buried in Inglewood Cemetery, California. They had a son named Thomas, my grandmother Adah Olive Lorimer's brother. I was born on June 3, my great uncle Tom's birthday. Three of us in five generations share June 3 in birth or death. According to my ninety-one-year-old mother, great uncle Tom had been a part of my life when I was a toddler but, regrettably, I don't remember him. Mom said he always called me a boy.

The baron had been a busy man with other properties and expenses so the castle at Sanquhar steadily began to deteriorate and crumble to a ruin, until 1895 when John Crichton-Stuart, 3rd Marquess of Bute, purchased it and attempted to restore life to his ancestral home. He'd already had great success with restorations at Cardiff Castle and Castell Coch in Wales. When he died in 1900, worked stopped.

Standing in a jumble of original stonework and crumbled renovation, I knew these ruins were my ruins. A chill ran down my spine and I glanced over my shoulder almost expecting a clandestine encounter with a hovering Lorimer apparition. But no such luck.

Historical Heroes

My castle made the history books. It was recorded that in the late 1200s William Wallace stayed in the castle on several occasions, probably with his Scots army of hundreds camped around the estate. More recent generations would know him as *Braveheart*, played by handsome Mel Gibson in the Hollywood portrayal. And let me interject that any man in a kilt is handsome. Now, portrayal or depiction is correct terminology or maybe even Hollywoodized, but I have to clear the air saying Hollywood really did a disservice to this historic character and the Scots in general. More about this soon in my rantings below.

First some history: William was born around 1270 to Malcolm Wallace and Margaret Crawford and had two brothers, Malcolm and John. They were a poor but knightly family and William grew up when King Alexander III ruled during a time of economic stability and peace. Then came political changes with Scotland close to a civil war, so Edward I, King of England, was invited by the Scottish lords to mediate. Before the whole thing could begin, he decided that they should call him Lord Paramount of Scotland. Edward proceeded to reverse the rulings of the Scottish Lords and summoned King John Balliol to stand before the English court as a common plaintiff. Malcolm Wallace refused to cooperate and sign the Ragman Rolls which was a collection of instruments by which nobility and gentry of Scotland pledged their allegiance to King Edward I of England in 1296. Malcolm was having none of this nonsense.

According to Lorimer family written accounts and those passed down generation to generation, it was said, "William was very tall with the body of a giant with strong arms and legs and very muscular." Back to my family claims later.

There are many books written about Wallace and that era, but it appears that he learned Latin and French from two uncles who were Catholic priests. When he was a teenager his father and older brother were killed by the English supposedly for not signing the Ragman Rolls.

William charged onto the scene and his recorded first act of defiance was the death of an English high sheriff in spring 1297, apparently to avenge the death of his wife, Marion. Then he joined the Lord of Douglas, and they carried out a raid of the town called Scone. Obviously a man with a giant and understandable grudge, Wallace led the army and won many battles, usually outnumbered by the English, because he knew the terrain which he used to his advantage throughout the summer months. On September 11, hiding out in a forest overlooking the bottleneck Stirling Bridge, biding their time just waiting for the perfect moment to ambush the English, the time was right and he and his warriors attacked a very well-equipped English army of over ten thousand soldiers and three hundred horsemen as they crossed the Stirling Bridge. Wallace's army's surprise attack caused the bridge to collapse, splitting the English ranks in two. Then the Scots, a scruffy bunch compared to the English, drove the confused English into the river. The Battle of Stirling Bridge was not only a thrashing but a major defeat. He was knighted by one of three Scottish earls, earned the title of Guardian of Scotland and gained quite a reputation for himself. The English were not amused.

My justified detour: The *Braveheart* movie didn't even include the factual bridge version but made up its own by calling it "The Battle of Stirling" lining up the armies across an open field, with blue-faced, kilted Highlanders charging at top speed toward heavily armored English troops. And the blue face paint? Where did that come from? It never happened. Read your history books to find that a millennium before Wallace, the ancient Romans did encounter war-painted fighters in Scotland, whom they called Picts (painted ones). Another mistake is that Robert the Bruce betrayed Wallace to the English. He did not. And William certainly did not impregnate the future King Edward II's French bride, who was ten years old, not yet married to Edward, and still living in France at the time of Wallace's death. Fake news, I say. There are problems with the movie's title too. No Scottish person ever referred to Wallace as "Braveheart," but actually it is the true nickname of the film's villain, Robert the Bruce. Bruce was hardly a villain and after his death a friend, Sir James Douglas, carried his heart in a small casket on a crusade to the Holy Land and during one battle, Douglas threw the heart at an oncoming army and shouted "Lead on, brave heart, I will follow thee!" There are more untruths or maybe artistic license in the movie but it did make for an entertaining fictional story with marvelous scenery. End of rant.

King Edward wasn't happy and in April 1298 ordered a second raid of Scotland where they looted Lothian and regained some castles but didn't draw William into combat. Edward was ready to strike again and paid Welsh longbowmen who swung the lead in their favor. The English attacked with the cavalry and sent the Scottish archers running. The Scottish cavalry also withdrew due to its outdated weaponry.

Edward's soldiers attacked but the Scottish were still able to cause major losses to the English. The spear-carrying Scots lost many men due to the archers and superior English on their horses. Wallace escaped but his reputation deteriorated and he went on the lam. Wallace resigned as Guardian of Scotland in September 1298, turning it over to Robert The Bruce, Earl of Carrick. His successors negotiated truces with the English, finally surrendering unconditionally in 1304.

William disappeared but about six years later he returned after being in Spain getting support. He became involved in more fighting but he dodged capture by the English until August 5, 1305 when a Scottish knight loyal to King Edward (unquestionably not Robert the Bruce) turned Wallace over to the English soldiers near Glasgow. They took him to Westminster Hall in London where he was tried for treason and for atrocities against civilians in war, "sparing neither age nor sex, monk or nun." They crowned him with a garland of oak implying he was the king of bandits. He responded to the treason charge, "I could not be a traitor to Edward, for I was never his subject."

Following the trial in England on August 23, 1305, William became so hated (but probably more likely feared), they took him from Westminster Hall to the Tower of London, stripped him naked and dragged him through the city at the heels of a horse. Several Wallace relatives witnessed the execution as they hanged William, and much worse followed, but it was too grisly for me to read or write. A plaque stands in the wall of St. Bartholomew's Hospital near the site of Wallace's execution, which I had read when we were in London two weeks earlier. I recalled the feeling of gloom I had while reading the memorial words.

Family lore passed down over the generations states that a William Wallace descendent married a Lorimer. But there is no way to prove it because there are no written accounts anywhere to show that William legally married his love, Marion Braidfute of Lamington. This seemed commonplace and most married but left no records for fear the English would find the papers or marriage certificates in churches, then locate the Scottish patriots' families and murder them all. Like other noble clan marriages at that time, marriages were kept secret because the English overlord claimed a first right of bedding any new wife before the new husband, and so men wanted to protect their brides. Most kept their marriage secret from the English as long as they could.

A 1995 adventure movie depicting another Scottish hero from the 1700s is *Rob Roy*. In 1713, Rob Roy MacGregor was wronged by a nobleman and his nephew and becomes an outlaw in search of revenge while running from the Redcoats. This movie affirms what horrible atrocities happened to families of Scottish nationalists by the English.

It is surmised that William was married to Marion and they had children who married and had children. One of William's grandchildren had a daughter named Elizabeth—Elizabeth Wallace to be exact. It became vitally important during this era to keep marriages a secret because after Wallace had been executed, any descendant would have feared for their life to claim Wallace as an ancestor. After William was murdered by the crown, the English disgraced his name and no one could risk being associated with him for about one hundred years. His children were at risk of execution. Many descendants of noble clansmen went into hiding for centuries.

My mother's cousin, Harry Alexander Snow of England, spent years chronicling and researching the Lorimer family history. He published and distributed his findings to the family.

This is what Harry wrote:

"Thursday, August 19th, in the year 1773, in the little Nithsdale town of Kirkconnel, near Sanquhar, a baby was baptized in the name of William, "lawful son to Robert Lorimer in Gavells." He was a sickly baby but survived. Apart from this glimpse, we know next to nothing about Robert and his wife, their own forebears, ages, the mother's name, whether they had other children or what they did for a living. All this is a closed book. Which is a pity, for these worthy folk were almost certainly the earliest Lorimers to whom our own line can be directly traced. I say almost certainly in the interest of accuracy because it cannot be proved absolutely that Robert of Gavells' son was that same William whose story now follows.

William of Knockenjig: This man, our certain ancestor was born in 1773. So was Robert's son. Knockenjig, like Gavells, lies in Kirkconnel parish, and as only one William Lorimer appears in the 1773 baptismal register for that parish, a single identity seems to be established.

When he grew up this William took to agriculture, like so many of the Lorimers. About 1805, when he was 32, William of Knockenjig married a young Scottish lass named Elizabeth Wallace. They had four or five children. (Editorial note: One child being Jean. She is my great-great grandmother, who married William Lorimer.) Some of "our" Lorimers have claimed descent from covenanting stock through that Colonel Wallace (Elizabeth's great grandfather) who met the covenanting leaders before the Battle of Bothwell Bridge in 1679. This gallant colonel claimed to have descended from the great William Wallace, whose name is forever enshrined in Scottish history."

None of this can be proved but at least we can now see family hints of the lineage and why my great-great-grandfather who immigrated from Scotland to Nebraska came to be buried in the Wallace clan tartan.

Since my mother told me her mother's father's grandmother, Elizabeth Wallace, used to tell him and all her grandchildren and great grandchildren about the infamous William Wallace, I am convinced that we are all William Wallace descendants. *Ancestry.com* proves I have thirty-one percent British blood coursing through my veins. Unfortunately, it doesn't break down what percentage is Scottish but their map indicates the majority is from Scotland with a bit dipping down into England. Therefore, I have chosen to believe that I am the great-great-great-great-great granddaughter of Sir William Wallace's great granddaughter, Elizabeth. I have Wallace blood in me and I have a copy of the Lorimer Family Tree to prove it. Now the burning question is: Am I the great-great-great-great-great-great-great granddaughter of William Wallace? It's way too confusing to figure that one out and I'm probably short three or four greats.

I found that another Scottish hero, Robert the Bruce, later becoming king, visited our castle on occasion, probably for protection and food. When his father died in 1304, Bruce inherited his family's claim to the throne. Bruce moved fast to seize command and was crowned King of Scots in March 1306, nine months after William Wallace died in England. Edward's forces defeated Bruce in battle and he had to go into hiding in Ireland but returned in 1307 and at Loudoun Hill beat an English army. Bruce defeated his other Scots enemies, destroying their English grip and ruining their lands. He had a series of military victories between 1310 and 1314 that won him control over most of Scotland.

He and William had been friends and served together against the English. In June 1314, Bruce defeated a much larger English army confirming the re-establishment of an independent Scotland. The battle marked a significant turning point—Scotland's armies could now invade England in the north. Bruce launched raids into the Borderlands. He also decided to expand his war against the English and created a second front by sending an army, under Edward his younger brother, to invade Ireland appealing to the native Irish to rise against Edward II's rule. There were good and bad Edwards.

But Edward II refused to give up his claim to Scotland. In 1324, the Pope recognized Bruce as king of an independent Scotland. In 1327, the English dumped Edward II for his son Edward III and peace was temporarily achieved.

King Robert the Bruce died in June 1329 and his body is buried at Dunfermline Abbey but his heart was interred at Melrose Abbey. He is still considered to be the most famous warrior of his time, leading Scotland during the first of the Wars of Scottish Independence against England. I always liked to think my youngest brother, Bruce, with his middle name William, was named for these Scottish heroes. The name William is scattered throughout my family for generations on both sides. My father's middle name is William and he had a Scottish grandmother. My brother Mark holds the middle name of Edward, I'm sure for the good Edward not the bad one.

Centuries later, Mary Queen of Scots frequented the castle. After her defeat at the battle of Langside, Lord Crichton became very loyal to Mary and hid her until she escaped across the River Nith heading to England. I found a blue metal sign that read, "Mary

Queen of Scots. Near this spot stood the town house of Lord Sanquhar who gave shelter to Queen Mary on the night of 13th May 1568, following her flight from the Battle of Langside. The Queen spent only one other night in Scotland before fleeing to England, never to return. Lord Sanquhar was punished for his allegiance to the Queen, and Sanquhar Castle was besieged and captured by Regent Murray's forces later that year."

Mary was also known as Mary Stuart or Mary I of Scotland and had been queen from December 14, 1542 to July 24, 1567. One can take days to read all the history about this extraordinary woman: murders, conspiracies, marriage agreements, illegitimate children, poisonings, beheadings, falling in love with her first cousin (not approved by the Catholic church), raids and wars, mysterious illnesses, nasty diseases, miscarriage of twins, abdications, attempts to regain the throne, hiding out in castles, betrayal by her sister and in custody for eighteen years, then executed. It was not an easy life for Mary. We have no Marys in our family.

In the 1780s, Robert Burns, the legendary Scottish poet and songwriter, had been a frequent visitor to Sanquhar. While renovating a farm in 1788, he often passed through on the way back to his wife, Jean, in Ayrshire. Burns called the town *Black Joan* in his ballad *Five Carlins* in which he represented the local burghs as characters. He would stay overnight at the Queensberry Arms on High Street. Supposedly Rabbie, as his friends called him, was a drinking buddy with my great-great grandfather William Lorimer. I only guess that he stayed at our castle as there is no way to verify this assumption. One story handed down over the generations is that Rabbie wanted his good friend William, along with some other men, to put up money to promote or publish Burns' book of poetry. Great-great grandpa evidently changed his mind probably thinking Rabbie's book would not sell. A big mistake. The story is that Burns called him a blockhead. I just want it to be fact that Rabbie slept at our castle and felt happy that someone involved in the arts, instead of war, was a frequent visitor. My father had a cousin from Montana named Robert Burns, called Bobby, whom I met several times as a child. He wasn't a poet but a scholar with bright red hair, sapphire blue eyes and bright red cheeks that jiggled when he laughed. I wondered if he was related to Santa Claus each time I saw him.

Our castle brimmed with centuries of famous patriots, or enemies, depending on which side one was on.

My Town

My research found that the name "Sanquhar" came from the Scottish Gaelic language meaning "old fort." It was established in an ideal location on the River Nith, at a crossroads for many centuries. Artifacts from the Neolithic period and remains of a few prehistoric British forts as well as traces of a Roman outpost have been discovered.

My family's small town sits north of Thornhill and just west of Moffat, in the Nithsdale valley close to ranges of hills on either side, the Carsphairn and Scaur ranges to the west and the Lowther hills to the southeast. The Southern Upland Way passes through the town on its way from Portpatrick on Scotland's western coast to Cockbrunspath on the east. I have concluded it is easier to spell than pronounce these names.

In the 9th and 10th centuries, Gaelic settlers came to the area from Ireland. The Scots-Irish people replaced the native Britons and became the dominant people for hundreds of years. In the 12th century, Norman occupation brought the feudal system of government and unhappiness became the norm with squabbling barons and sheriffs who ruled the land for several centuries. Because of its location near the English border, it was in a constant state of turmoil as groups raided each other across the border lines.

Sanquhar became legally recognized by the crown as early as the 15th century and made a royal burgh in 1598. It is the place where the Covenanters who didn't want to conform and be Episcopalians signed the Sanquhar Declaration renouncing their allegiance to the King. There is a monument on Main Street.

Despite the political unrest in the area, agriculture began to flourish in the early 18th century. Local industries came into their own, particularly coal mining. Other industries that depended on coal, such as weaving, carpet making and forges, began to appear. Wool had been a vital trade in the coastal trading towns since early days and Sanquhar developed as an inland market place. The Sanquhar Wool Fair, held annually in July, regulated the prices for the south region. The unique two-colored pattern glove started here. Many poor farmers supported themselves with extra income from these sought-after knitted garments. During the 18th century the life of a weaver became enviable. They earned good wages and worked at their looms indoors, mostly at their homes. They could work whatever hours they wanted, and could take time off in autumn to help with the harvests. Towards the end of the 18th century, however, progress in technology made the home shops less profitable and many of Sanquhar's weavers found themselves looking for other jobs.

Sanquhar itself prospered through the late 19th and early 20th centuries and had a public school as early as 1793. A famous Scottish architect designed the tolbooth in the middle of town. Most towns had one used as a council meeting chamber, a court house and probably a jail. The tolbooth was one of three essential features in a burgh along with a mercat cross (market) and a church. In 1800, about two thousand three hundred people lived in Sanquhar, a few thousand less when we visited.

The town has the world's oldest curling society formed in 1774 with sixty members, so obviously curling became an extremely popular sport. James Brown, who wrote the history of the town, is also credited with writing the rules universally used for the sport. There were tournaments where the prize was a bag of grain. The winning team would get the food and distribute it to the needy in town. The only thing I knew about curling had come from watching the winter Olympics and a long-time friend and past coworker, Darrel, who was a curling champion in his younger years when he lived in Edmonton, Alberta. To me it seemed like a person with a broom pushed a round rock down an icy track to make it into a circle. Darrel gladly enlightened me on the intricacies of curling that the normal person would never see.

Finished prowling around the ruins, we returned to town and while in a local gift shop looking for handmade gloves to take home to my mother, I learned and saw first-hand from Murdina, the shop owner, more about the distinctive two-colored patterned knitting. She told me the history that the upland valley of the river Nith had been good sheep country with soft water for processing wool and already had roads following the river to markets in central Scotland. I loved her accent and she patiently spoke slowly so I could grasp everything she had to share. I commented on her lovely name and she told me it meant "sea warrior." She said the weavers used only needles or wires that they made by hand.

I asked her how a pattern was created. She said probably from seeing other patterns like plaids and flannels that were already popular. And it seemed perfect timing because ladies of that era all were wearing gloves as they were sensible and fashionable. The use of dyes for more colors and different patterns than had been used and seen before made the dozen styles of geometrically patterned Sanquhar gloves widely popular.

She said that examples of the gloves knitted by people in Sanquhar were gifted to the local museum, showing the value placed on the gloves and the skills of individual knitters. Through oral history, the story is shared about how the traditional patterns were taught. There are a small number of family names in Sanquhar which reappear in connection with the glove, ensuring the survival of the patterns. And the school became involved in teaching the knitting of the gloves in its needlework classes. The Sanquhar pattern glove is still knitted today by a few dedicated, skilled knitters carrying on a practice, and I was buying a pair for my mother. I knew every time she would wear them, she'd think of her family ties.

While shopping for silver jewelry and souvenirs in another shop, looking at items with thistles, a salesperson named Aileen shared some folklore with me. I told her our names were similar and she asked me how I got my name. I told her it is a combination of my father's first name, Del, and one of his sisters, named Colleen. She said hers had not been a handed-down family name but it meant "ray of sunshine." She told me that there are legends surrounding the thistle and said the durable weed has always bloomed across Scotland but it wasn't until the 13th century that its place in the country's symbolism and written record began. One of the best-known thistle legends takes place in the mid-13th century during a surprise invasion by the soldiers of the Norse king at one of the towns on the west coast. The story is that after coming ashore this Viking force planned to creep up on the Scottish clansmen and overcome them while they slept. This amount of secrecy required that they go barefoot. Unfortunately for the invaders, a soldier's bare foot came down hard on a Scottish thistle and his cries of pain were enough to wake the sleeping Scots. Leaping to their feet, the clansmen charged into battle and the rest is history. Legend has it that because of the brave role the flower played in the outcome of the battle, the thistle became the national emblem. By the 15th century the Scottish Thistle had been adopted as a national emblem. Sounded totally truthful to me.

She also explained that the Scottish flag is really azure, not just blue but more of a cobalt, with the X-shaped cross being a hint of silver but often depicted as white. After spending a week in Scotland, I could see the difference between plain blue and white that I thought were the colors when crossing the border. Now azure and silver; my perspective had changed.

I learned during our time in Scotland that these people know the value of a dollar (or pound). This doesn't mean they are stingy, just careful about spending, and expect value for their money. They are honest and forthright and will say what they mean but not with cruelty. They are patriotic. They are practical and down to earth. Many have a strong belief in the supernatural. They appreciate artists, poets, writers and musicians. They are hardworking and success has many times come on the backs of those who have gone before them. They know how to have a good time with singing, dancing, eating and drinking. They appreciate and enjoy their food, especially red meats. And they also like a "wee dram" of whisky.

Roots

After picking up souvenir treasures, our last stop would be at the local parish church, Saint Bride's, where we would find some of my relatives. I knew my great and great-great grandfathers were buried in their adopted country of America. The church, constructed in 1827 to 1828, seemed a modest size gothic church with its four-spiked pinnacle towers and clock guarding the cemetery. The sanctuary had been paneled with dark wood and supported by square columns with a low pulpit below an arch. The leaded windows were clean, making it easy to view the grounds.

Out in the grassy cemetery, most headstones were two to eight feet tall, many with Celtic crosses engraved into the stone. I walked along row after row of headstones with hand-carved names and dates, some with explanations about who they were and the significance to their families. Most had common first names such as Mary, John, James, Ruth—biblical sounding to me. But the last names were the most interesting. It seemed many clans were represented. I was thrilled to find my great-great grandmother Jean Wightman's headstone and even though it was difficult to read due to years of weather and decay, I put a piece of paper over the top and colored in the wording with a pencil.

It read "In Memory of Jean Wightman spouse of William Lorimer late farmer in Auchencrow who died 21st January 1853, age 46. Also of the said William Lorimer who died at Hazel Hall, Nebraska USA, 28th October 1875 age 67 years. Also of Robert Lorimer, their son who died 6th November 1895 age 65." The engraving would go to my mother.

I found a prominent memorial to my great-great-great grandparents, Alexander Wightman and Jean Bell. Another stone listed George Lorimer dated 1693 and died in 1767, the earliest of all the Lorimer records in this particular cemetery. I knew there were other little cemeteries in the area with more memorials of my family but we didn't take time to explore more. I'd read that a James Lorimer was born in 1603 and died in 1683. All of these people gave their lives for the future generations and I felt honored to be part of the lineage.

Driving out of Sanquhar I promised myself I would return one day. As we departed the town, I saw a sign, "Thank you for visiting Sanquhar."

I whispered, "No, I thank you." I became teary once again.

Epilogue

Twenty-one years later, exactly on July 10, purely coincidental if anything really is coincidental, I returned to Sanquhar via train from Glasgow. Two days of this fourteen-day journey would be spent soaking in my heritage vibes and rediscovering my roots. Accompanying me on this trip was another Joyce, who had traveled with me to Europe and Iceland and was game for any foreign adventure. It seemed appropriate that a second Joyce was enjoying Scotland with me since my first Joyce escorted us twenty-one years earlier.

My heart skipped a beat the first time I watched the scrolling reader board on the train displaying the various town names along our route. Each time I read Sanquhar I got more anxious with anticipation. When the train briefly stopped on its way south, I saw the official Sanquhar sign. I was there! This town was too tiny for an official train station with a building. There were just a few benches with pots of flowers. On this trip, I would spend more time in this charming village than two hours, twenty-one years earlier.

Meandering down the hill on the sunny morning, rolling my one piece of royal blue spinner luggage, my first sight was of a large, yellow stone home with an olive-colored door with ivy and vines growing up the left side. The next home had the exact same color door but more ferns and other greenery encroaching on both sides and over the top of the doorway. The first recognizable landmark to greet me was the Tolbooth. The clock on the tower read 10:04. We were standing on one street with three different names. First, it's Glasgow Street that becomes High Street then into Castle Street. There's still only one main road. The Tolbooth sits proudly in the middle where two streets split. There are two identical dark brown doors, one on each side of the building with a door squeezed in between. I could see through the middle door and out the back because it was open and only protected by ironworks and potted begonias. Two stone staircases were adorned with a black iron handrail and seven pots of more begonias flowing from hanging baskets. From the street level up about fifteen steps to the front door and official entrance, there were more pots of healthy begonias, about every color in the rainbow. Now the clock read 10:28; it was time for exploration. Across the street was the Nithsdale Hotel on the High Street section of the road complete with friendly, helpful staff and accommodations that could use a facelift. The meals were delicious and hearty. I knew I wouldn't get lost as Saint Bride's Parish Church was at one end and the castle at the other, at most one mile apart.

The first order of business was getting to my castle. Walking down the road I read in a store window, "Sanquhar Pattern Designs" that boasted of original knitwear, handcrafted with love in Sanquhar, the home of the historic pattern with a wide range of items available in merino wool. It wasn't open on Mondays.

I stood beside the "Welcome to Sanquhar, Please Drive Carefully" sign. There were no wildflowers growing helter-skelter at the base but planted marigolds sprouting their yellow and orange colors in a well-manicured stone planter. Though not visible from the road, I easily found the well-used, narrow dirt path marked with a plaque explaining the history of the castle and ruins. Walking between knee-high green grass and prickly tall purple thistles, ducking under low hanging tree branches and skirting around grazing sheep who didn't know or care this was my family's home from hundreds of years before, I spotted the castle ruins in the distance. The weathered gray stones were brightened by sunbeams that bounced off the walls creating interesting shadows. Gray clouds hovering over rolling green hills in the distance matched the stone wall color. Standing as close as possible to my family castle, I was kept at a distance as it is surrounded by a chain link fence protecting humans and sheep from falling crumbling stones. While gazing at the lush green rolling hills that my forefathers left behind when moving to Nebraska -- Nebraska, seriously? -- my heart felt like it broke in half. Tears started flowing. It was so sad they didn't make it as far as Oregon where at least the scenery and climate were similar. Colorful little wildflowers swayed in the gentle breeze as I walked around as much as I could. There are no tall trees remaining but shorter scrubbier ones. The ground was very uneven with high and low spots that made exploring difficult. I was lucky not to twist an ankle when I stepped into a hole that was hidden, covered over by years of uncut grass. I found no precut holes in the fencing to climb through nor did I have wire cutters with me. I took dozens of photos from all angles.

I discovered another trail that led to the old caretaker's cottage, also marked with "Danger Keep Out" signs, warning of harm and probably death. I stopped to pet an attentive brown horse, seemingly curious about who was intruding on his turf and probably wondering why I wasn't carrying a treat. As I pet him, he nuzzled my neck and shoulder. I wondered if he was a descendant of the horses from the castle. I was beginning to wonder if everything, including sheep, might be descendants. Then I wondered if I might encounter a long-lost cousin in town.

Strolling back on a side street I discovered a small church with a bright red side door. Pink roses were in full bloom situated in a garden surrounded by a stone wall. On the way to the historic post office, there was a turquoise-painted house with a navy blue front door. It was squeezed between a stone house and a painted yellow one. It really stood out. The Tolbooth Cottage has a double red door. Again, I was enamored with all the colorful doors. The post office now has only one door serving as the entrance and exit and is painted shiny bright red. The other side of the building is an apartment and its door is the matching red. Also added is a "Tourist Information" sign above the brass box that letters can be slipped through. The post office is also the only gift shop. Standing proudly in the corner is a bright red, seven foot tall postal box, about as tall as the telephone booths, those typical red ones you see all over Great Britain. It was for decoration only. I sent my mother a historical photo of the street from the 1800s imprinted onto a postcard and which included the official stamp reading "The World's Oldest Post Office," obviously their claim to fame. I purchased several items for my mother including a woven jute bag trimmed in red, and printed in black on the front proudly boasting:

The World's Oldest Post Office
Sanquhar Post Office
In Operation Since 1712

It includes a design of a man riding a horse and with his left hand, blowing a trumpet. The man has a big bag the length of his entire torso strapped to his back and it's full of something, maybe wool. I decided I needed to have one also, assured that we'd be the only two people in Oregon with this bag. Maybe even in the United States.

While having lunch at our hotel, as it was the only restaurant in town, there was an elderly couple who greeted me. The woman asked about the purpose of my visit as they don't get many visitors in their village. I gladly explained why and my brief family history. Could she, would she, be a long-lost relative? She sure looked like she could be with her fair complexion, blue eyes and white hair. She asked my family name and I replied, Lorimer. She said she'd lived there seventy years and was over ninety. Now, she was a reliable source. She shook her head and said that the last Lorimers moved away some years back. Sadly, there would be no long-lost relative encounters for me. I wondered silently if I could adopt her as my own kin.

My afternoon stroll on the way to Saint Bride's Parish Church took me by the police station with one car in the front. It was a silver Ford station wagon type vehicle with fluorescent yellow painted on the side and a sky blue thistle logo on the hood. I took a photo for my youngest brother, the sheriff in Linn County, Oregon. I decided to go in and introduce myself and ask permission (after the fact) to take some photos. The sign at the door read: "Opening Hours Monday-Friday 9:00 a.m.-5:00 p.m. Reception closed between 12:30 p.m.-1:30 p.m." As I was about to push open the door, it opened for me as a police officer greeted me, fortunately wearing a broad smile and a green uniform. I told him my story and he said he saw me taking photos. It was absolutely fine. His name was Officer John Carter and he was pleased to meet me. He sent warm greetings to my brother, a fellow law enforcement officer. He gave me some tips on what else to see in the area.

The church looked exactly the same as well as the ancient headstones and some more recent ones in the adjoining graveyard. Unfortunately, I had forgotten to look through my photo album of my first trip to see where my great-great grandmother Jean was buried. I started the circle to the left and for about a half hour wove in and out reading most headstones. Then I had a flashback recalling a large tree and her being somewhere near it. From the back of the cemetery I recognized the tree just to the right of the church entrance. If I'd only started on the right instead of the left, I would have seen it immediately. The wording is almost impossible to decipher so I was glad I had placed a piece of paper over the top and with a pencil traced the wording twenty-one years earlier. I talked with great-great grandma Jean thanking her for her part in my life and why I was visiting. I told her about my sweet grandma and my dear mother. I choose to believe she heard me and was pleased.

That night I walked around neighborhoods of large stone homes with bright colorful doors and well-kept front yards about the size of an eight by ten throw rug. "Yards" to us and "gardens" to them, were lined with petunias and marigolds, rose bushes flourished and hydrangeas came in all colors not just blue ones like we have in our backyard. One grass green door had the name Crawick View over the top. The Dunlugas' door was ebony. The Barr View door was sapphire blue. Colorful laundry hung from lines in backyards. Birds chirped, bunnies hopped, and I wondered if Sanquhar had become a town for people over sixty. It just seemed peaceful and the perfect place to retire. The loch is almost in the heart of town but nestled in a pocket of woodland. I pictured my ancestors picnicking on Sunday afternoons with other parishioners from Saint Bride's Church. My guess is they ate lamb. Way-too-eager mallards waddled up the bank from the lake's edge, ready to attack for bread or crackers, none of which I had. I spotted a squatty duck on the bank with a rust-colored head, gray and white body, and black tail. My *Waterbirds and Nearshore Birds Guide* indicated it was a wigeon. A Greylag goose, mostly gray with a yellow bill, wasn't far from the Canada geese family. We have an overabundance of Canada geese in our region so I wasn't nearly as impressed with them as the swans, whose type I couldn't determine at my distance but they were either a Bewick's swan, Mute swan or maybe even a Whooper swan. I had left my binoculars in the room so had no positive verification. Walking farther we discovered a bridge and crossed the River Nith. Four children were playing along the slow-moving, shallow river. I was sure they could walk across. The water seemed gentle and welcoming. Standing on the bridge looking up and down the river, I knew my relatives had played in the water, maybe bathed or even drank from it. Walking back, there was Saint Bride's towering above rooftops.

That night for dinner I had delicious fresh salmon with a lemon sauce, mash (really potatoes), and broccoli cooked perfectly. The dessert menu included Banoffee Pie (what?), apple pie, sticky toffee pudding, chocolate fudge cake, cheesecake and all the above delectable delights included your choice of ice cream, pouring cream or custard. Additionally, there was Knickerbocker Glory (didn't ask) and a trio of ice cream. After walking 16,395 steps that day, I decided to splurge and asked for the, surprise me, Banoffee Pie. It had a graham cracker crust, a layer of whipped creamy custard, topped with sliced bananas with heavily drizzled caramel over everything including the generous scoop of vanilla ice cream. Each bite got better and better instead of, frequently, the other way around.

After a brief walk, we returned to our upstairs room after a day of emotional exploration. About ten o'clock I watched the sunset lighting up layers of clouds in shades of blue, gray, gold, orange and yellow from the hotel's third story bay window. As I was dipping a teaspoon for the third time into a jar of "Wilkin & Sons LTD Tiptree Lemon Curd, Fruit Growers and Preservers since 1885" (don't judge and you wouldn't if you've ever tasted it—best dessert ever even though it's really a spread for toast), movement caught Joyce's eye. "Quick, come see," she almost shouted. Two men turned down the road, each leading a Shetland pony, one blond and the other medium brown, just like a dog on a leash, as if it was an everyday occurrence. Maybe it was in Sanquhar.

The next morning our train to Edinburgh wasn't leaving until eleven o'clock. We retraced our steps around town waiting for breakfast to be served at our hotel which was included in the nightly price. The sun was shining directly on the Tolbooth causing the baskets of hanging orange begonias to look like they were glowing. Taking a closer look, I discovered small, delicate trailing white flowers. A black door with a rounded top was encased in painted white molding against a gray stone wall. I couldn't tell where it went or if it really opened. I liked the door-to-nowhere idea. In one field, tiny purple flowers were lit up by rays of sunshine, and with the green rolling hills in the background and blue sky with random puffy white, happy clouds, the scene looked like something my painter friend, Steve, should try. Sticking up through a centuries-old rock wall poked the familiar purple thistle. The only thing dark was my shadow. To my right was a layer of thistles, a moss-covered stone wall, and behind it were tall purple flowers but clearly not foxgloves. Later I would learn it's a useless herb. (We say "erb," they say "herb.") At the loch, the water was so still I could see the reflection of tall and shorter clumps of bushes. The ducks that had been sleeping on the bank spotted us again even though we were quiet and careful not to rouse them, so we retreated before being attacked and felt guilty that once again we forgot to bring a treat. It was almost breakfast time at the Nithsdale, and walking back on the main road it was apparent this sleepy little village was still asleep. Breakfast included cereals, porridge, poached eggs on toast, scrambled eggs on toast, omelette (spelled the Scottish way), or the Full Breakfast that included egg, bacon, sausage, tomato, mushrooms, tattie scone, black pudding, tea or coffee. I took the full Scottish breakfast minus the black pudding. I clearly recalled my first educational experience twenty-one years earlier. Blackcurrant jam or orange marmalade was plentiful.

Full from breakfast, we packed up, said our thank you's and farewells then rolled our luggage up the hill to the train station while glancing down on a part of the cemetery and church close by. Pretty sandstone homes, the church, blue sky, birds chirping, green hills dotted with sheep and hardly any vehicle noise made me wonder if Sanquhar is the Scottish version of Mayberry. I blinked tears away thinking once again about my ancestors leaving this little spot of heaven. I felt I was leaving home for a second time hopefully to return again one day.

Trip Tips:

Don't forget to study up on the country you are visiting. There are many inventors and artists who had their start in Scotland. I found a little book called *Braw Stuff Fae Scotland*, a fascinating wee collection of Scottish people, ideas and discoveries from Neolithic times to the modern day, to be terrific conversation starters:

Buick Motor Company. David Dunbar Buick, born in Arbroath in 1854, emigrated with his family to America two years later. He subsequently settled in Detroit and founded the Buick Motor Company in 1903 which passed out of his ownership three years later, and was ultimately owned by General Motors. Thirty-five million cars have been produced which carry his name.

Adhesive postage stamp. Claimed to have been first proposed by James Chalmers of Montrose in 1838.

The bicycle. Not only is Scottish blacksmith Kirkpatrick MacMillan thought to be the inventor of the modern bicycle, but he was also involved in the first recorded road traffic offense when he knocked over a pedestrian in The Gorbals.

Decimal point. John Napier introduced the decimal point into common usage.

Douglas fir. Named after David Douglas from Perthshire, the celebrated botanist and explorer born in Scone. In his short life, before dying under mysterious circumstances in Hawaii in 1834 at the age of thirty-five, he introduced over two hundred forty species of tree, shrub, flower and herb to the UK.

Fingerprinting. Dr. Henry Faulds from Beith published the first paper establishing the uniqueness of everyone's fingerprints in 1880.

Lawnmower. Alexander Shanks, like David Buick, was from Arbroath and is credited with creating the first 'horse-drawn grass cutting machine', which was trailed in 1894. Be sure to visit the Arbroath Lawnmower Collection when you're in town.

Modern steam engine. Greenock-born James Watt, repairing an engine in 1763, realized that he could make it far more efficient by adding a separate condenser, thus requiring less fuel and generating more power. He received a patent for the modern steam engine in 1769. He also developed the concept of horsepower, and the electrical measurement, the watt, was named after him.

Don't forget items in your carry-on for your long flight like earplugs or noise cancelling headphones, inflatable pillow, a shawl or large scarf that works well as a blanket or to block out light, eye mask, sanitizing wipes, compression socks, sleep aids, food and water, pen, paper and notepad or journal, chewing gum and one set of extra clothing. And don't forget your prescription medications.

Don't forget your passport and make a copy to put somewhere else in your luggage. Make a copy to leave at home with a trusted friend or relative.

Don't talk too much but keep it small talk unless you are friends. Scottish people prefer indirect communication because they don't want to accidentally insult anyone.

Don't ask them to repeat themselves if you don't understand them. And don't speak slowly or loudly when talking with them; they are not deaf.

Don't talk about politics and religion unless you are asked, then state your opinions and don't get in a debate about Scottish independence.

Don't call what you think are mountains, mountains. They are called Scotland hills. So if someone asks if you want to go for a walk in the hills, be warned, it's something much larger.

Don't get hit by a car or bus. Like the rest of the United Kingdom, they drive on the opposite side of the street. Look right, left and right again before stepping out in the street.

Don't forget good walking shoes for meandering out to castle ruins, on the ocean shore or uneven cobblestone walkways.

Don't forget a rain poncho for any time of year; forget the umbrella and don't complain about the quick-changing weather.

Don't tell them how you've heard it always rains in Scotland.

Don't astound them with your lack of Scottish geographical knowledge. It's north (above) of England on the same island including Wales.

Don't take a photo of someone unless you ask first.

Don't make remarks about Scottish people as they are extremely proud of their country.

Don't talk about England; they have a long history and don't always like one another and for heaven's sake, don't call them English.

Don't ever call a kilt a skirt. If you are purchasing a kilt, be prepared to spend several hundred dollars because they are handmade and constructed with over eight yards of material.

Don't complain about bagpipes; sure, they are loud but it will stir something deep within your soul.

Don't skip the national foods.

Don't avoid people; be polite and greet everyone with a hello. Always say "please" and "thank you" as the Scots are polite and may become offended if you do not mind your manners. If you bump into someone, say "sorry."

Don't complain about not spotting Nessie nor talk about your views of the Loch Ness Monster or share you lack of belief in faeries.

Don't avoid trying to say some words in Scottish. Even though they speak English, they have their own dialect with a thick accent and their own words. Get a list of commonly used words and practice before you go and don't say them wrong. Don't pronounce "Loch" like "lock." Review on YouTube.

Don't ever snap your fingers or wave your hand at a waiter in a restaurant.

Don't ask to take home food as leftovers. If you can afford to eat out at a restaurant, you can afford to buy other food to eat later.

Don't forget a hostess gift if you are invited to someone's home; a gift from home or a bottle of whisky always works.

Don't mention that you don't like the host's food; try to eat everything that is on your plate. Just don't take too much if you don't think you will like it.

Don't burp or wipe your nose at the dinner table; excuse yourself.

Don't worry about tipping at a restaurant because it is automatically added to your bill as a service charge. This is common practice in most countries around the world except the U.S. You can leave a bit more if the service is exceptional but it is not expected.

Don't forget to smile. The Scottish are gracious and kind and as long as you smile and mean well, you will get along just fine.

Don't forget most British words are the same in England, Ireland, Northern Ireland and Scotland. And what Americans call the second floor of a building is the first floor in the U.K.

Don't forget the metric system is used almost everywhere in the world so weight and volume are calculated in metric. A kilogram is 2.2 pounds and one liter is about a quart. Temperatures are generally given in Celsius. Twenty-eight Celsius is a perfect eighty-two degrees to us. Twenty is sixty-eight and zero is our thirty-two degrees.

Don't forget clothing and shoe sizes are different.

Scottish words that might help:

Afters means dessert.

Bap means small roll or sandwich.

Bampot (bam-pot), eejit (ee-jit) means idiot also interchangeable with cyclists.

Barry (ba-ree) means splendid.

Bevvy (bev-ee) means drink.

Bloody means darn or damn.

Brilliant means cool.

Cairn means a pile of stones.

Cheers can mean good-bye or thanks and also a toast.

Cider means alcoholic apple cider.

Close means an alley leading to a courtyard or square.

Coach means long distance bus.

Crabit (krab-it) means grumpy. Don't be this way.

Digestives are graham crackers but round like cookies.

Druth (drew-th) means thirsty.

Eilean means an island.

Fortnight means two weeks.

Gallery means a balcony.

Greeting (greet-ing) means crying.

Haver (h-ave-er) means you talk too much.

Kirk means a church.

Knickers means ladies' panties.

Loo means toilet or bathroom.

Nappy means diaper.

Neeps means turnips.

Mannie (man-ee) means a little man.

Mate means buddy for a boy or a girl.

Mean means stingy.

Mental means wild or memorable.

Messages (mess-a-gzz) means groceries.

Motorway means freeway.

Nought means zero.

Och (o-ch) means oh, as in "never mind."

Off-license means liquor store.

Pasty (PASS-tee) means crusted savory meat pies that are delicious instead of a sandwich.

Plaster means a Band-Aid.

Pitch means a playing field.

Public school means a private or prep school.

Rasher means a slice of bacon.

Scotch egg means hard-boiled egg wrapped in sausage.

Sleeping policeman means speed bumps.

Soda means soda water not pop.

Spotted Dick means raisin cake with custard.

Wheesht (whee-sht) means be quiet.

Tapadh leat (taap-u-let-th) means thank you usually shortened to Ta.

Towpath means a path along a river.

Whacked means exhausted.

Zebra crossing means a crosswalk.

Zed means the letter Z.

Try to stress the first syllable on every word. "Chaidh" is pronounced as "Hy." Note that a "T" sounds like a "Ch." A "Bh" sounds like a "V" and a "DH" sounds like a hard "K."

Before visiting the U.K. you may wish to purchase a British-Yankee vocabulary guide: it's educational and humorous. And for goodness' sake, buy a well-respected travel authority's book on Scotland like *Rick Steves' Scotland*, and read every word.

"Travel opens your eyes and your heart."

Deleen Wills

The Walnut Door
Are We There Yet?

What? Windsor Castle again? Peering down seventeen thousand feet from my United Airlines window seat at the multi-hued green English countryside, I began recognizing the same historic looking buildings and lush landscape. I turned and said to my husband, "I know I've seen Windsor Castle three times." He didn't say a word but just looked at me with that familiar "you are exaggerating" look.

"Ladies and Gentlemen," the captain announced in a mellow distinguished British accent, "We are orbiting and awaiting approval for landing at London Heathrow. We expect to begin our approach in three-quarters of an hour. Sorry for the inconvenience but with the delay departing the U.S. we're in a queue for the gate." Nauseatingly polite and calm, why couldn't he just say we'd be going in circles for another forty-five minutes? Forty-five minutes sounded much better than three-quarters of an hour to me. I glanced at my husband and gave him the stare and said, "See, I told you I've seen Windsor Castle three times." "Yes dear; you're right again." I noticed a tinge of sarcasm but let it go. Fidgeting in my seat, he and I both knew I was now orbiting too. By my schedule I realized part of our travelling group had already landed and were awaiting my arrival as their trusted, organized, always-punctual group leader. I felt fearful they would be wandering aimlessly like lost sheep around Heathrow airport without their shepherd. What could I do but try to breathe deeply? Too late to pop a Xanax.

For the past year, I had been organizing, orchestrating, and now finally escorting a group of attorneys and their families for ten days, staying at Mansfield College, one of dozens of educational institutions that are part of massive Oxford University. The lawyers would study English Law and have some unique legal experiences all pertaining to their profession. Their families would be tourists as excursions had been designed just for them. I even allowed time for eating and sleeping but other than that, the itinerary was fairly full.

It looked great on paper. I had planned this program five thousand miles away using only email (a new invention) and a telephone, keeping in mind they were eight hours ahead of us from the west coast. A small part of my job in alumni relations at a law school included organizing travel programs. We had two flights from PDX (Portland, Oregon) with some others flying from California, Alaska and the Midwest. Supposedly, we would all arrive within thirty minutes of each other, get on our awaiting Pearce's motor coach, then drive a couple of hours from Heathrow to Oxford and Mansfield College. Again, it all looked great on paper and I had already ticked off boxes on my master check-off list: Passports, check. Luggage, check. Passengers, check.

Our flight from PDX left on time and we met up with other travelers at LaGuardia, on the east coast. My husband and I, plus one-third of our group, were scheduled on the first flight out, planning to arrive earlier than others. Having a bit of extra time would allow me to figure out how to use an English telephone (twenty years ago, way before cell phones) to call the bus driver who would be waiting in a coach parked several miles away, watch for other stragglers and get us on the way.

The announcement over the PA system at La Guardia broadcasted that our flight would be delayed one hour. There were ten of us on the first flight. The later flight, which now left on time, had twenty of our group. Of course, it was packed full and I couldn't switch my husband and me to that flight. "Relax," I said out loud to myself, repeatedly. I felt flushed and my temples were throbbing, all because of the out-of-my-control situation. I told myself to "stop it" and went for a walk, or more like pacing, around the airport. Finally, waiting the hour plus a bit more, whatever the issues were, they had been remedied. We boarded and popped over The Pond while I took a nap. And now we were orbiting, a new word in my vocabulary regarding flying—orbiting, circling, looping, circumnavigating—it seemed like it took forever.

But we finally landed and, feeling rejuvenated, I sprinted down the corridor while my weary husband lagged behind pulling one carry-on. We went through a long immigration line as several other foreign flights arrived at the same time. Brits seem to do well standing in queues but not Americans. I had plenty of observations and comments that I mumbled to myself: Why don't they hire more staff during the busiest time? Why isn't there any air conditioning? No one answered nor did anyone welcome me on my first visit to the United Kingdom. The unsmiling, bushy eye-browed elderly immigration official who peered over his dinky reading glasses teetering on the tip of his nose, asked if I had come for work or pleasure. I decided to select one answer because, even though answering the word "both" would be the most honest, it might be confusing, create the necessity for an explanation and we were already late enough. Obviously, they didn't understand this was my first time stepping foot on British soil and I felt a bit giddy and talkative, a dangerous combination for me. I kept my answers to one word.

We got our passports stamped in another new country and moved through the necessary protocol of arrival in a foreign land. We met up with weary passengers from the other flights, found our motor coach and smiling driver, Clive, who made up for the obviously not-happy-with-his-job immigration officer. Fortunately, Mr. Grumpy would be the exception to the friendly, polite and kind Brits we would meet. Clive would be our chauffeur for our time on the road. Away we went, finally. The slightly swaying back and forth sensation on the bus ride caused most to fall asleep with their heads nodding like bobble-head dolls but I felt too keyed up with anticipation. Not only was the one-year's-worth of planning coming to fruition, I greatly anticipated meeting a new friend I'd acquired while planning this adventure. We'd spoken by telephone numerous times and used the new email communication system. She was the bursar's secretary and until this trip, I'd never heard of a bursar. Her responsibilities were vague and vast. She not only dealt with all of his duties but was also responsible for all students from the day they arrived until they left, dealing with their accommodations as well as their studies. Plus, she had been assigned the responsibility for planning summer conferences. Her name was Pearl; the name of the birthstone of the month I had been born. She had already become a gem in my book for being so patient, explaining all the customs and rules and warnings of the college's minimalist accommodations.

Oxford, England and Mansfield College

When we arrived at the outskirts of Oxford in late June 1996 it seemed like any other medium-sized town but it quickly transformed into what appeared to be a step back in time. Had we time-traveled back to the 1600s? I had only seen Oxford in television programs and movies. As our charter bus maneuvered through narrow streets lined with oversized colleges and universities, Clive nicely pointed out historical sites where we would soon be visiting. He told us of prominent Oxford alumni such as Bill Bradley, basketball player and past U.S. congressman; Edwin Hubble, astronomer and scientist; Dudley Moore, actor; King Edward VII; George Stephanopoulos, news anchor; J. Paul Getty, art collector, just to name-drop a few. He seemed proudest of America's forty-second president, Bill Clinton. In fall 1968, Clinton was one of thirty-two American Rhodes scholars. At twenty-two years old, Clinton studied there for one year. Clive said he'd seen on television during election time that Mr. Clinton had admitted to at least one embarrassing experience at Oxford—he smoked marijuana, although he said he did not inhale. Clive laughed.

Soon we approached a college on tree-lined Mansfield Road. The sunshine reflected off the limestone buildings causing a golden hue and warm homey feeling—my first sighting of Mansfield College. Hidden down a quieter avenue but only a few blocks from the main road and hub of all activity, it would be a very convenient location. I left the travelers basking in the sunshine as I went in search of the kind woman who had been helping me arrange this experience for the past year. After a warm hug and welcome from Pearl, who seemed immediately like a long-lost sister, she escorted us to our lodgings at Mansfield College, Oxford University, Oxford, England, Great Britain. I was finally here. I felt ecstatic to be in a country where I had a few roots on my family tree.

At the first building on the left (called a staircase instead of a dormitory or residence hall), through the arched yellow stonework we pushed open a heavy exterior door before my husband and I entered room 102 on the first floor. The interior walnut door to our accommodations looked similar to others. This would be our home-away-from-home for the next ten days. Our L-shaped quarters were sparsely appointed with two twin beds, two desks, each with a reading lamp, and two wooden straight-backed chairs with no cushions. On each desk sat one rough, small bath towel and one hand towel, plus a bar of hotel-size white soap. I had a black dial telephone on my desk with no operating instructions. Because of my conference responsibilities and possible interruptions, I volunteered to take the bottom of the L closest to the door. A partial wall separated the two areas. My side had thin slats built into the wall where

I tucked a mirror and toiletries. The electrical outlet in the middle of the wall beneath the shelves wasn't at all convenient, especially with the desk across the room. The only mirror affixed on the wall above a miniature sink happened to be on my husband's side of the L. We had stayed in a youth hostel once in Amsterdam, our one and only time in a hostel; this seemed to be one star above. I opened an armoire about the size of our refrigerator at home and I found no hangers. However, I'd discovered this before on trips and always carried one dozen wire hangers with me, the kind you get for free from your dry cleaners. I draped three blouses per hanger and used them all, mostly for me. These were no-frills accommodations and I concluded that Oxford students were serious about their studies and the types who didn't care much about creature comforts. I wondered how our American students would cope with such plain and simple lodgings.

There was one "bathroom" in the corridor that occupants from two rooms on each floor would share. Right next door was a second equal-size room with a toilet and sink. The "bathroom" had a sink, a mirror above it and a shower. Neither had electrical outlets. We learned quickly that a bathroom is for bathing. We were there to be students soaking up English law—and sightseers gleaning new insights—accommodations didn't matter that much. And for me, a dandy place to work for the next ten days.

While unpacking, the overhead lights went out as I heard a little scream from across the hall. Even though I had told travelers repeatedly about using adapters and converters, someone had already forgotten and melted the plug of her curling iron, complete with a spark from the socket. The blown fuse was replaced quickly and the electricity came back on. This would be the first but certainly not the only apology for my group. I felt slightly better when staff nicely said that this was common, especially the first day with guests suffering from lack of sleep and jet lag.

One tradition my husband and I do when arriving in a new town is ride either the "Guide Friday" or the "Hop On/Hop Off" bus to get the lay of the land, and that's exactly what we did. Plus, we needed to stay awake. I knew how to thwart jet lag—no napping but staying awake and active until night fall. Then after a full eight hours of sleep, we'd be feeling great. Seeing All Souls College, with its twin towers flanking the Common Room, Christ Church and the Bodleian Library built in 1435, was the first stop where we hopped off after taking the entire tour route. It seemed like we were in an English television program. The *Brideshead Revisited* series, about two very different young men becoming friends while at college at Oxford, had just played on our public broadcast station (PBS). I became more interested in the architectural wonders and surroundings than the soapy program. I sobbed through the tear-jerker movie, *Shadowlands*, based on Oxford academic C.S. Lewis, brilliantly played by Anthony Hopkins. The love of his life, played by Debra Winger portraying real-life American poet Joy Davidman, dies from cancer. It had been mostly filmed in scenic Oxford. The Queen of Crime, and one of my favorite authors, P.D. James, had been born in Oxford. I'd read several of her murder mysteries where her characters jump back and forth between London and Oxford. This had been the only Oxford I knew, until now.

Ninety-eight, ninety-nine, one-hundred, and at one-hundred-three I lost count as we climbed the old wooden stairs to the top of the Sheldonian Theatre. From the ornate cupola we had an incredible panoramic 360-degree view. Following the printed map starting in the south we saw University Church of St. Mary the Virgin, Merton College Chapel, Christ Church Cathedral, Tom Tower, Lincoln College Library, Exeter College, Nuffield College, Wesley Memorial Church, Church of St. Michael at the North Gate, Balliol College, the Taylor Institution, Radcliffe Observatory, Trinity College, the New Bodleian Library, Keble College and Wadham College. Husband Mark pointed out our temporary home, Mansfield College, Manchester College, Hertford College, St. Catherine's College, John Radcliffe Hospital with the college tower and chapel next to it, St. Edmunds Hall Library, the Bodleian Library, All Souls College and the Radcliffe Camera completing this most impressive circle of history, life and education. The only thing they seemed to have in common besides being old, was the color—all goldish. The entire remarkable, historic town from this eagle-eye vantage point seemed to be laid out at our feet for us to explore and appreciate. Now I really felt like I had been dropped into the middle of an English movie.

After the city tour and being duly wowed by architecture and structures, we returned to campus. I felt pretty special to be living on a campus at Oxford University. Standing in the middle of "our" campus, we could see the residence halls with each room's windows facing the plaza. The main college buildings enclosed three sides of the large U-shape, with a circular lawn. At a quick first glance, I also spotted a picturesque, Old-World looking chapel with stained glass windows. I knew explanations would come later on an official campus tour.

Pearl informed us all at the Welcome Reception, where we were served assorted nibbles (our version of appetizers) and Elderflower (a lemon and vanilla cordial), that the College had been founded in 1838 as Spring Hill College, Birmingham, a college for Nonconformist students. In the 19th century, although students from all religious denominations were legally allowed to attend universities, they were prevented by statute from taking degrees unless they conformed to the Church of England. In 1871, the Universities Tests Act ended all religious tests for non-theological degrees at Oxford, Cambridge, London and Durham Universities. For the first time the educational and social opportunities offered by Britain's leading institutions were open to all. Pearl continued explaining that Spring Hill College moved to Oxford in 1886 and was renamed Mansfield College after its biggest donors, George and Elizabeth Mansfield. The Victorian buildings were completed in 1889 and Mansfield was the first Nonconformist college to open in Oxford. The College accepted only male students until 1913 when the first woman had been admitted.

Pearl continued by adding that during World War II, over forty members of staff at the Government's Code and Cypher School (GC&CS) moved to Mansfield to prepare British codes and cyphers, while the GC&CS members at Bletchley Park worked to decipher the German enigma codes. Years later I would watch *The Bletchley Circle*, a television series on PBS set in the early 1950s about four women who had worked as codebreakers at Bletchley Park. I recalled what I had learned at Mansfield two decades earlier about their secret work. I recognized many familiar locations in London and Oxford.

In 1955, the College became a Permanent Private Hall within the University of Oxford, and in 1995, Mansfield was awarded full college status, Pearl continued educating us. She noted that Mansfield was a relatively young college in comparison with other schools, each having their own stories of their early beginnings and history. The chapel contained a unique assortment of stained glass windows and statues showing leading characters from Nonconformist movements, including Oliver Cromwell and William Penn, among many others. In 1940, while lecturing at University College, future British Prime Minister Harold Wilson married Mary Baldwin in Mansfield's chapel.

Because of its Nonconformist roots, the College still had many strong links with American schools. It has a tradition of accepting about thirty "Junior Year Abroad" students from the United States every year. They come to study in Oxford for one academic year and have full access to its libraries and tutors. Pearl noted that twenty-eight students from all over the United States had been on campus that year, but no one from the west coast. They had just left and returned home for their senior year. She explained that the main building had been constructed starting in 1887 and was finished one year later. It housed the main library and the law library, to which our attorneys had full access. We would use the main building most of the time because of the Junior Common Room, Middle Common Room and Senior Common Room, where we would hold legal classes. Pearl pointed to the Principal's home. This title is equivalent to a college president in the U.S. She concluded the enlightening campus tour by saying we were welcome to enjoy the grounds at our leisure.

I headed for the Principal's home that had been constructed with the same yellow limestone. The lovely two-story house with rounded bay windows accommodated a terrace on the second level. I attempted peeking in the leaded, beveled glass windows but could see only delicate lacey curtains, the ones where the residents could see out but peeping guests couldn't see in. The yard, or what they call a garden, exploded with many colorful types of flowers evenly placed to give it a true English-garden-look. I strolled around the corner of the house staying on the walking stones carefully obeying the sign to "Please Stay Off the Grass." Again, it seemed so polite adding the word "please" to everything. I ambled through a black iron trellis smothered in lavender wisteria into a flourishing rose garden. The first row of well-manicured roses was the color of persimmons with each center bleaching out to a lighter orange. I read "Betty Harkness" printed on a little plaque mounted on a post. A second row of vivid red roses with pink undertones had curiously been named "Benjamin Britten," a fun name to say three times. Separate from the others was a single bush of all-white roses that looked almost translucent, like crepe paper. The sign read "Claire Austin." Several bushes with soft pink roses seemed appropriately named "Lady Of The Mist." There were three bushes with bright yellow roses that for some reason had been named after royalty, "Lord Mountbatten." Not only were the roses award-winning, the air smelled like perfume from Paris. I loved these English-sounding names. I declared my favorite to be the light pink rose with apricot center, jam-packed with petals almost as dense as a peony. The plaque read "Celtic Pride." I didn't have a clue what the names of my few rose bushes at home were but I would certainly label them something British-sounding when I returned. And as I was curious about the rose named Benjamin Britten, Pearl explained he had been an English composer, conductor and pianist and a central figure of 20th century British classical music.

We had several charming and amusing Mansfield staff taking care of us during our stay and one colorful character in particular. Whereas Mike had the job of the Senior Porter, Hugh was the Lesser Porter—I hoped he didn't have a complex due to the word 'lesser' in the title. While visiting the porter's lounge for one of my regular responsibilities of checking the pigeon-hole mailboxes, Hugh and I were chatting about his years at Mansfield and he told me he had been the drummer for *John Mayall & The Bluesbreakers*, whom I'd never heard of, and he had appeared on their first two albums, the second of which featured Eric Clapton, whom I had heard of. He later formed the band *McGuinness Flint*. He looked the part with his long, flowing gray hair pulled back in a ponytail tied with a piece of red twine. Duncan, the bursar, held the position of the financial administrator of Mansfield, and was responsible for sending bills and making payment plans. He gave us a tour of the library. Robin, the steward, was not only responsible for the domestic staff and the dining room, he seemed like an omnipresent overseer or guardian who appeared to be taking care of all sorts of issues that might have been much worse had he not handled them. He was most helpful with a medical situation where a mother and adult daughter weren't seen for several days. And replacing fuses several times.

Firsts

Every morning we were treated to a "full English breakfast," or a "fry-up," in the baroque-looking dining hall. Most of us had never experienced a full English breakfast so it was humorous on that first morning watching the reactions of my band of lawyers and their families checking out the eggs, beans (much like our pork and beans from a can), grilled tomatoes, cubed fried potatoes, mushrooms, limp bacon, mystery sausages, and toast with assorted jams. The toast came out cold and the tea piping hot. The English seem so sensible and to-the-point. The toast had been heated at one time to cause it to become brown but there had never been a promise that it would or should be hot or even warm when served. Evidently, the role of cold toast was merely a means to an end so one could legitimately smother something with soft butter before layering lemon curd, jam or marmalade, which would be amply applied. We got used to cold toasted bread and I slathered it with homemade lemon curd or orange marmalade daily. I snuck, or so I thought, a spoonful of tart, yet sweet flavorful lemon curd each breakfast minus the toast. Mysteriously on day three a jar and a spoon, only one, turned up in our room. The first two mornings everyone politely ate what had been placed in front of them. By the third morning we were kindly asking to skip certain parts of the meal.

Down the street on the corner of Mansfield Road and Holywell Street, about a five-minute stroll, sat the slightly unconventional sandwich shop called, "The Alternative Tuck Shop." The curved storefront had been painted bright grass green with clean white trim. Displayed in the window were the most delicious looking pastries ever. They didn't need to do any promotion or advertising; this window display said everything to promote the place. It became clear very quickly why there was usually a line out the door to this little establishment.

When I walked in the first time, I was surprised to see a display of Kettle Chips for sale right in front of the check-out counter. This company was from my hometown in Salem, Oregon. How in the world did Kettle Chips find its way to this little eatery in Oxford? A nice young man at the counter told me the chips are second best to the UK brand of Walkers Crisps which they also sold. I bought multiple bags of Walkers since I could have Kettle Chips anytime at home. The salt and vinegar were my favorite but we tried several types before coming to that conclusion. Ready Salted (made sense to me), Prawn Cocktail, Marmite, Smoky Bacon, Sour Cream and Chive, Tomato Ketchup plus several more were sampled. I figured out the best times to frequent my new favorite place in the world before the crowds arrived.

Menu items were changed daily and posted on the black chalk board behind the service counter. Sandwiches like hazelnut chocolate spread, cheddar cheese, and peanut butter and jam were the traditional, boring choices. We didn't have enough hours in the day to try the multiple variations of chicken, cheddar, avocado, sausage, tuna and cucumber, salmon and cream cheese, turkey with curry; the list and combinations were almost endless. I picked up, as often as possible, brie and avocado sandwiches and fresh fruit, sometimes with chicken, turkey or bacon. The second visit, waiting to try something additional, I discovered the most scrumptious triple-layer bar I had ever tasted in my entire life. The bottom layer was a quarter inch buttery shortbread, the middle was a taller layer of non-gooey caramel, topped off with a thick semi-dark chocolate layer. It made perfect sense this delectable delight was called "Caramel Shortbread Squares." I bought these by the dozens and happily supported the local economy. Writing this story now makes my mouth water for those scrumptious delicacies.

While our attorneys were in class the morning after our arrival, retired archeologist David Sturdy led us non-law tourists on a walking tour: in and out of secret passages, along ancient walls, spying into cramped quarters on narrow boats on the river—seeing his Oxford, through his archeologist eyes. We stood under the Bridge of Sighs and having seen the original in Venice a decade earlier it appeared a pretty fair replica, and took a group photo. We stopped by the market and picked up sandwiches, fruit, crisps and cookies for a picnic along the river. While drinking wine that David had brought along, he shared architectural chronicles and accounts, nothing hearsay from him. He seemed in his element; so were we.

The grounds of Mansfield College conveniently near the center of Oxford, were also close to the University's parks and the River Cherwell. The college shares a boundary wall with Wadham College. That afternoon Mansfield staff, particularly Robin, the steward, and Nick, the development officer, attempted to introduce us to cricket in the park across the street. Nick seemed on a personal mission to educate Americans on his favorite pastime. I'd spent some time with him talking about fundraising, sharing the differences in our systems, how donations were handled and the tax implications. We thought it would be terrific to do a job swap for a year.

Cricket is a bat and ball game played between two teams of eleven players on a cricket field. That's the easy part. The field is vaguely similar to our baseball field. However, cricket has a long rectangular pitch area of dirt with a wicket and a set of three short wood stumps at each end. The wicket is formed by the three stumps and the ball sits atop the third stump. This was not a game with a pitcher, batter and some outfielders like we are used to. Our pitcher is their bowler who is bowling the ball to a batsman, or batswoman, or should it be a batsperson? Nope, it's batsman, didn't matter male or female. The equipment used is a cricket ball, cricket bat, wickets, and various protective equipment. It really would be have been best and safest to have leg guards and padded gloves. We had none. Before we attempted to not get hit by the hard cricket ball made of cork covered in leather, one of the players gave us a brief history starting with fashion and equipment. Breeches or trousers had belts with metal clasps; beaver hats were replaced by tall hats that were replaced by one's own cap. Colored shirts were worn—some with high collars and others wore a rather large bow tie. Footwear was usually the black "Oxford" shoe. The players we saw were all wearing white. Nick explained that the designated batting team attempts to score as many runs as possible while the other team is in the field. The bowler throws the ball from one end of the pitch to the other toward a set of wooden stumps, in front of which stands the batsman guarding the stumps with the bat.

Standing in a circle listening intently to the instructions, Nick asked who'd like to bat first. My intrepid group, or so I thought, seemed to simul-taneously step backwards leaving me by myself. My brave friends all pointed to me; some friends they were. It was explained that all I had to do would be to prevent the ball from hitting the stumps by using the bat. Protect the stumps, hit the ball, and score runs. The bowler was supposed to prevent the scoring of runs and strike out the batsman. I felt like the sacrificial lamb. But I wanted to make America proud like in the Olympics. They showed the proper stance and I was permitted to take a couple of swings with the unusual sized, flattish bat. After the second strike, I connected with the ball and ran to a base but was out and I never questioned why. The entire game seemed very confusing. Everyone had a chance at being the batsman and some got to try their hand at being the bowler. Another new experience plus a lot of laughs for the memory books. That evening I was formally presented with a cricket bat that all the Mansfield staff had autographed.

The next morning while our attorneys were hard at work gleaning more about English law, some of us toured open houses on different campuses. We also went into the Bodleian Library with its massive arched front door etched with the coat-of-arms from several Oxford colleges. "The Bod," as it's affectionately called by locals, is packed full of journals, newspapers, magazines, music recordings, maps, prints, drawings, manuscripts and books, with over twelve million items. Since we were officially students of Oxford, even temporarily, we gained entrance. All colleges at Oxford have their own libraries but "The Bod" is the main research library and one of the oldest in Europe.

That afternoon, again being encouraged by the Mansfield staff to do something outside our comfort zone, we went punting. I did wonder about their snickers as we marched off towards Magdalen Bridge on the River Cherwell. There are two rivers in Oxford. The first is the Thames, that meanders for over two hundred miles through ten counties and all the way to London, dumping into the Thames

Estuary where it meets the North Sea. The second river is the Cherwell, pronounced "Char-well." Confusing us further was the issue that within the boundaries of Oxford the Thames is also called the Isis. While renting our punt, I glanced around and saw no Edwardian men in white slacks poling a daintily attired companion along the meandering river like in the movies. Turned out punting was really nothing like our canoeing or rowing, both of which I had done. A punt is a flat-bottomed boat with a square-cut bow, designed for small rivers and shallow water. And it looks bigger than it really is. But a punt is not a canoe or a boat or a gondola, which uses an oar. The punter, when he knows what he is doing, usually propels the punt by pushing against the riverbed with a pole. It didn't seem too tricky, and watching others, didn't look all that complex or difficult.

Jerry's wife and Pat's roommate declined the venturesome opportunity. Maybe they had a premonition. Our first blunder was overloading the boat with five healthy Americans. One member of our adventurous, naïve and totally unprepared fivesome, was a self-assured outdoorsy attorney. At six foot eight inches and two hundred seventy pounds plus, Dave was a big man, even goliath-like. Jerry perched himself sitting low in the very front of the punt with Pat in front of him, who dangled her hand in the cool river. Mark and I sat side by side facing Jerry and Pat with Dave standing behind us as the punter. I could only see him when I glanced backwards—once was enough. We were sitting so low in the water with only about a half inch to spare before The River Cherwell would be joining us in our punt. Our punter wobbled back and forth several times trying to gain stability, almost falling overboard and tipping us all out. But he somehow regained his steadiness as we sat there white-knuckled, clinging onto the side of the punt acting like we were having the time of our lives. The jargon "Are we having fun yet?" was not used then but as I write this, I have no doubt my husband would have uttered those words. There were no life jackets provided and I didn't know how to swim. We twirled in circles two times until he got the knack of it. None of us volunteered to give him a rest; even though huffing and puffing and sweating profusely, the poor guy got no reprieve from us. With lush trees and shrubbery lining the banks, more than once he got smacked in the face with low hanging branches. Still there was no offer of substitution from any silent, petrified riders. Not daring to turning around, I could only look straight ahead at the faces of Jerry and Pat with their grimaced lips, and eyes either tightly closed or round as the one pound British coin, a reflection of what was going on behind us. Punting, like many other sports, is not as easy as it looks. As in rowing, you soon learn to get the hang of it but it takes practice, which none of us had. We learned later that it can take weeks or months of practice before one can punt with dignity and without getting water up one's sleeve and everywhere else.

Clearly we weren't the only first-timers on the river that afternoon as we could tell from the laughter and swearing and watching several punts going in loops as we did. After the near-drowning punting incident, we lunched along the river watching the white swans and giggling at the other punters looking as silly as we did a short time earlier. One of my favorite slogans is, "Adventure Awaits, Go Find It." We were doing just that. Down the river we could see thin barges and quaint houseboats. They were actually called narrowboats, designed to fit the skinny canals. A few sunbathers were relaxing in lounge chairs on the top of a red narrowboat. It seemed some were used as rentals for leisure and some were actual homes. It looked like a great adventure to me as I nudged my husband and he said out loud so I would never forget it, "Maybe sometime we should try a river cruise in Europe but on a longer boat."

That evening for dinner, since we were on a roll for trying new exploits, we went to an Indian restaurant about a twenty-minute stroll from Mansfield. It came highly recommended again by the Mansfield staff, although at this point I was beginning to somewhat question their judgment. I felt dubious at best. I'd never heard of or thought about trying Indian food as we certainly didn't have any restaurants serving this nationality of food in our hometown, even though it is the state capital of Oregon. The only ethnic food we had were Mexican restaurants, which were plentiful. With hand-scribbled instructions from the Mansfield jokesters, we spotted a small sign that read "Tandoori Restaurant" and someone commented that meant chicken in Indian. There appeared to be a restaurant perched on top of a Tandy electronics store.

I pushed open the white banged-up door and we hesitantly started up the two flights of stairs to places unknown. However, with each step our pace quickened because of the heavenly aromas. We boldly ventured in promptly greeted by a nice-looking, mature woman who said, "Welcome and Hello," but didn't seem to know any more English than those two words. Her younger accomplice helped seat us and decipher the menu—the pictures of entrees helped too. The scents wafting from the kitchen smelled delicious. Plates piled high with fascinating-looking food being delivered to other patrons look scrumptious. Plus, we were starving after expending all the energy and calories punting. The waiter suggested we begin with the naan, their famous flat bread, which came from the oven warm and golden brown. The bread went along with spicy mashed-up beans called hummus plus a mint, cilantro chutney yogurt dip. Then a steady stream of food was delivered with appropriate time between the various courses, beginning with a plate of cubed cheese they called paneer—it tasted milky with just the right mix of lemon juice, and a big bowl of cucumbers in a yogurt dressing with lemon and mint. Their yogurt wasn't like I had been accustomed to eating in a little plastic container with flavors of blueberry or cherry with fruit at the bottom. Who knew yogurt could be so varied and appetizing? Pots of Indian spiced tea called masala chai, came piping hot and flavorful. We sampled a peppery cabbage with ginger, hot chilies, garlic and onion. We started a guessing game trying to figure out what all the spices were. Next was a bowl of ghee rice and taking a nibble I could clearly taste licorice with cloves, chilies for a zesty bite, along with a bay leaf and chopped onions. The proprietors seemed gratified that we were entertaining ourselves with these first-time delicacies. One asked us what we thought we were tasting. When I replied licorice in the rice, our helpful waiter said it was anise. It felt like the spices were doing jumping jacks on my taste buds.

Tandoori chicken came out on multicolored orange platters piping hot and it looked finger-licking good. However, no one else in the restaurant appeared to be eating the chicken with their fingers like we did at home. It had been prepared with a light yogurt and spices, again lip-smacking. We didn't lick our fingers even though we wanted to, badly. For the grand finale, dessert, they brought out the house specialty, called kheer or rice pudding. It tasted somewhat bland after all the flavorful food we'd just devoured. We thanked our hosts, new friends from another foreign country now living in their adopted country, England, for their luscious food, hospitality and patience and promised to return once more before our trip ended. In fact, we went three times overall, each time taking different suspicious travelers from our group to introduce them to the yummy food, cordial family and staff. Wary friends became converts.

While preparing for the trip and determining what the lawyers should see and do, it was important that I remember they were bringing their families who would want to have non-law experiences. I had inquired with the national tourism board and dis-covered a non-practicing barrister, Tom Hooper, who'd given up his law practice to become a guide. But he wasn't just any guide—we had a real life Blue Badge Guide, the highly esteemed level of guide through the Institute of Tourist Guiding. I was be-ginning to really love the British nuances.

I learned quickly that this is a really big deal and Blue Badge Guides are the official, professional tourist guides of the United Kingdom. They wear a Blue Badge to indicate their professionalism. All Blue Badge Guides must pass the Institute's exams and study for up to two years at the university level, taking a comprehensive series of written and practical exams which qualify them to become Blue Badge Tourist Guides. After learning about what the Guides went through for testing and certification, I thought their well-deserved Blue Badge should be a medallion or Olympic medal.

Tom dressed professionally and wore navy slacks, a collared shirt and different tie with some entertaining and amusing pattern every day. One day he showed up wearing a tie with hot air balloons because my husband and I owned and flew one in Oregon. Did we ever luck out! Not only was he smart, he knew the ins and outs of English law and had personality plus with that dry English humor. He wasn't bashful to share quips about his country, the royal family and political satire; however, always respectfully. He'd say something funny and I cracked up but no one else except my husband seemed to get it. Tom would simply look at me with furrowed or raised brows and roll his eyes, mumbling something about "Yankees" for my benefit. One morning Tom said a first for me: "The light is on but nobody's home." He was describing someone in our group to a tee after several incidents triggered the accurate assessment. He seemed proud to share an occasional well known saying crediting the Brits for it. This was just the beginning of him interjecting jargon such as: a dog is a man's best friend, a friend in need is a friend indeed, take with a grain of salt, a rolling stone gathers no moss, keep your chin up, a fish out of water, all bark and no bite, dog days of summer and don't count your chickens before they hatch.

Another time, when describing the architect Christopher Wren's buildings in Oxford, one traveler in our group asked, "Isn't he the character in *Winnie the Pooh*?" Tom politely answered, "No, madam, that's Christopher Robin." I felt mortified at the comment from someone in our esteemed group. Later we privately had a good laugh and Tom said that wasn't the first or second time someone (from America) had asked that very same question, maybe confusing a Wren with a Robin; it made me feel a little better. I blamed everything on jet lag.

Countryside Encounters and Follies

Tom stayed with us for the week and the next morning started sunny as we drove through the countryside to Warwick Castle. Within one hour the clouds rolled in and gave us a sensational storm complete with earsplitting cracks of thunder and intense bolts of lightning. It felt creepy with the thunder echoing through tunnels and dungeons of the best medieval castle in Great Britain. And I knew it must be haunted.

The State Rooms brought to life the over-the-top and stuffiness of aristocratic society in the 7th and 8th centuries. In the Chinese Bedroom, Tom pointed out the life-size Daisy, the Countess of War, in full regalia with her maid kneeling on the floor hemming the Countess's gown. In the Great Hall, entire knights in shining armor (minus the human beings) stood on a red tiled floor with fancy tables and chairs and lavish handcrafted armor. Tom guided us from room to room describing the history and what we were actually looking at. In the State Dining Room, against a backdrop of opulent and detailed tapestries plus a chandelier with thousands of crystals like I'd never seen before, I imagined Queen Victoria dining here. Tom laid out the extravagant Victorian lifestyle of the Earl of Warwick before our very eyes. The torture chamber, dungeon and spooky ghost tower with ancient uneven creaky doors didn't let us forget the consequences of wicked behavior—a great deterrent for sure. Inside the castle were also actual size horses draped in blankets, saddles and head pieces to protect them in battle. Each room depicted what actually happened centuries ago. It took hours to wander through the best castle I'd ever seen. The castle overlooks sixty acres of grounds and gardens and the noisy peacock haven, with sizeable, colorful cranky birds. The Victorian rose garden popped with a myriad of flowers in full bloom and we strolled on a nature walk around the lush river island. Attending a Renaissance fair here would be awesome.

As we headed to Blenheim Palace, Winston Churchill's birthplace, we made a brief stop not far from the Palace at St. Martin's Church in Bladon. It's the cemetery where Winston Churchill is buried along with his family. It had been his wish that he be buried close to his family home. Here are also the graves of his parents, his wife Clementine and his children Randolph, Diana and Sarah. He died at age ninety. The cemetery overflowed with lush bushes and trees. Tucked away in the corner by a little building stood a five-foot tall, brilliant pinkish red hydrangea bush with the blooms about the color of a pomegranate. At home, ours were only blue or purple and sometimes white.

A short distance from me stood a distinguished, even debonair, tall, gray-haired man wearing a blue blazer with a swanky neckerchief tucked professsionally down into his open-collared white shirt with well-pressed and sharply-creased gray slacks. He spoke in a semi-hushed voice with a trio of visitors standing near Churchill's marker. A single strikingly deep red rose in an unremarkable vase sat at the lower right-hand corner of the white marble grave. As my group moseyed around the cemetery, I stepped in a little closer, feigning interest in reading and photographing the highly regarded ex-prime minister's modest headstone. Eavesdropping, I heard the man say in a baritone voice that he was the younger brother of the Duke of Marlborough—whoa, as in THE Blenheim Palace Marlboroughs. His older stepbrother, Jamie, had the prestigious title of Duke. He kind of chuckled, not really a genuine laugh, when he asked if they'd heard the term, "Heir and the Spare" and said, "I'm the Spare." He seemed forthcoming and comfortable about his misguided, immature and irresponsible stepbrother with his well-publicized and photographed drug issues, extravagant expenditures, almost being disinherited and many other sensational tabloid escapades that were, unfortunately, mostly accurate. He told the visiting trio that, as a member of the Spencer family, they were distant relatives to former Prime Minister Winston Churchill. Loitering much longer might be too obvious so I moved slowly away to another gravesite as I was reminded that extraordinary

125

experiences like this only happen when one travels, thus reinforcing wanderlust—a great desire to travel and roam about. I couldn't wait to share this insider's scoop with my band of explorers and Tom.

We drove a very short distance into the tiny town of Woodstock and our first sighting of Blenheim Palace, a monumental country house that looked aglow with warm cream to golden colors. Tom said it is actually bigger than Windsor Castle or Buckingham Palace and most notably known for the unexpected, early arrival of Winston Churchill in 1874. I say "early" because we were told he had been born one month earlier than the normal full-term baby. Coincidentally, his parents were married eight months earlier. All documented facts but back in those days, called rumors. Blenheim had been the main residence of the dukes of Marlborough over the centuries and the only non-royal, country house in England to hold the title of palace. It had been built between 1705 and 1722. Following the completion, it became the home of the Churchill, and later the Spencer-Churchill family. At the end of the 19th century, the Palace was saved from ruin by funds gained from the ninth Duke of Marlborough's marriage to American railroad heiress, Consuelo Vanderbilt. It wasn't uncommon in the 1800s and 1900s for rich American families to ship their daughters to Europe to marry and gain a title. Hundreds of American daughters were sent to Europe and many marriages ended badly but some withstood the time and pressures of a completely new culture. I'd watched a program on American heiresses and it didn't reflect well on parenting skills, selling their daughters to the highest bidder with a title, in my humble opinion. Decades later, watching *Downton Abbey,* the same situation was true and based on a real-life situation, but they lived happily ever after.

We crunched our way across the parking area, and looking down to see what created such a peculiar sound, I noticed crushed shells. It turned out that the stones used in the Palace are unique because they are full of fragments from large fossil sea urchins and sand dollars. We toured the interior of this famous palace full of the secret passages and I pondered, if the walls could talk, would they share hundreds of years of whispers, rendezvous, murders, schemes and plots? The history of the home was quite intriguing and didn't need any embellishment from my imagination. Family portraits dozens of feet tall lined the ballroom walls. The Green Dining Room had a complete table setup and looked as though it could feed fifty at a moment's notice. There were hundreds of pillars, scores of fireplaces, countless white columns and crystal chandeliers. I always remind myself to look up at ceilings and this time saw many frescoes and paintings. But one room in particular felt quite creepy as it had a giant blue eye and a massive brown eye peering down at me. The Great Hall was another major area of interest—the birth room of Sir Winston Churchill.

In the west and south corridors there were three State Rooms plus the Red Drawing Room, and the Green Writing Room with the famous Blenheim Tapestry, showing Marlborough as he accepted surrender after the Battle of Blenheim. Tom was brimming with information and it was fabulous having him share history and insight instead of reading a brochure. There were two libraries—the Long Library, and yes, there was a short one as well, both having stunning interiors and many thousands of collectible books. The Grand Salon, with black and white flooring, contained the dining table surrounded by dramatic red high-backed chairs, and laid out with spotless table linen, well-polished crockery, and candlesticks galore. There were several dining rooms all different and impressively appointed. No way would I want to be polishing all the candlesticks in this place; that job alone would take several employees. Outside were gardens: the Italian Garden with fountains, the secluded Secret Garden where we only saw the sign, and the Temple of Diana (not Princess Diana who we knew and loved). This is where Winston proposed to his wife-to-be, Clementine. We walked on a bridge across a stream to The Column of Victory and viewed the splendid Grand Cascade waterfall that flows from the Great Lake. A maze had been created out of alphabet-shaped hedges plus a giant chess game that we elected not to attempt. We made a snack-stop at the Water Terrace Café and sampled typical English fare of teas, crustless sandwiches and cakes, and tried estate-produced jams and honey. I wondered what it would be like to stay for a night in this historic palace, so important and meaningful to my ancestors, as some of my roots are in England. My mother had cousins in the area but I didn't have the time to look them up. I still regret that as they are long gone now.

Oxfordshire, shires are much like our counties, encompasses vast countryside with lakes, rivers, streams, farms and mysteries. On our return trip from this day of historic castles, we detoured down a narrow lane lined with hedges of fuchsias and stopped at the Rollright Stones. The first thing we spotted was part of the King's Men stone circle, one of three monuments that make up the Rollright Stones. The Stones is a complex of three Neolithic and Bronze Age megalithic monuments near the little burg of Long Compton on the borders of Oxfordshire and Warwickshire. The three monuments, made of local limestone, are known as the King's Men, the King Stone, and the Whispering Knight. They are distinct in their design and were built at different periods. Amazing.

I felt relieved and safer that we were visiting in broad daylight as we paraded around and around the stone circle quietly waiting for something mystical to happen—maybe a premonition, an epiphany, teleportation—anything? Nothing, not even an electric jolt or a buzz except by a yellow and black, fuzzy bumble bee pollinating a clump of knee-high, bright yellow flowering rapeseed that produces canola oil. In the distance were more acres of the yellow flowers and purple flowers on tall stems which Tom said were flax or linseed, used to make linseed oil. We learned historical plus agricultural information today. Looking across the rolling hillside, we could see parcels of bright red poppies gently swaying in the breeze. I loved the vivid countryside bursting in yellow, purple and red. For some reason, I felt very much at home.

That night, Vivaldi's *The Four Seasons* was being played at the Sheldonian Theatre. As we walked around the ring-shaped theatre we looked up as a hot air balloon floated peacefully over the town. What a vantage point they had! We owned *Valley Sunrise,* a checked, upward spiral seven-colored, patterned hot air balloon packed away in our garage at home. Unfortunately, on this trip we didn't have the time to check into going for a ride.

Tom again shared his wisdom that the Sheldonian had been designed by Sir Christopher Wren, not Robin, at age thirty-one, who at the time was a professor of astronomy at Oxford. This became his first significant work. The building took five years to complete in the mid 1660s and is the hall with the most ceremonies in the University. We had unreserved seats which were tight, wooden and straight-backed but had a perfect view of the pipe organ across the room. These seats were not made for anyone over five foot two inches and one hundred pounds. The pipe organ touched the painted ceiling which reminded me of the ceilings painted with frescoes in Italy. I saw a light blue sky with a brown cloud and the cloud had pink cherubs tumbling from Heaven. What I read in the Sheldonian brochure was: "The paintings, oil on canvas, were painted by Robert Streater, showing figures tumbling among clouds, a tortuous allegory of truth descending on the arts and sciences, while envy, rapine and ignorance are cast out of the university." There is always more than meets the eye, especially with art.

A small group of musicians presented *Four Seasons,* each giving musical expression to a season of the year. Vivaldi wrote it about 1723. I could swear in the middle section of the Spring concerto I could hear a barking dog in the viola section and birds during the summertime on the violins. I became enthralled with the fast-slow-fast movements and thought I could envision falling leaves in autumn and snow falling in winter. It had been an enchanting evening. As we moseyed back onto campus, the outdoor lights shone on the yellow limestone, glowing like gold.

Almost every day on our way to the open market we walked under the faux Bridge of Sighs. One morning we were cutting through a different direction and some police officers (bobbies) were putting out orange cones separating pedestrians on the sidewalks from the street traffic. Obviously, something unusual was about to occur. We delayed our food purchase to see what might be up. Soon a nondescript black boxy Bentley drove down the road and sitting in the back seat were Nelson Mandela and Prince Charles. I waved and Nelson looked right at me, smiled and waved back. Husband Mark turned to me and excitedly said, "Did you see that President Mandela looked right at me and waved?"

Honestly, I didn't care one bit about Prince Charles because he and Diana were just divorced. I wasn't happy with him after the recent news announcing he had become officially involved with Camilla, evidently done with hiding his infidelity. He didn't count on my quest to see royalty. He seemed to have gotten everything he wanted—two heirs. Most of the British I'd met weren't happy with him either because they loved Diana. I really, really, really wanted to see Princess Diana or Queen Elizabeth or actually anyone from the Royal Family but Charles. Everywhere we went I kept an eye out for the royal black Bentleys that they were known for being escorted in. Even with several visits to England in upcoming years I never saw the Queen or any other royalty.

However, six years later in autumn 2002 while on a four-day cruise with a one-day stop in Victoria, British Columbia, two serendipitous encounters would clinch my loyalty for all things royal. I had gained a new respect for the Queen of England by now as she had gone through tremendous heartache the past several years with multiple tragic family situations plus the monarchy wasn't held in the high esteem as it once had. I felt sorry for her. Now seventy-six-years-old, in my opinion she'd done the best she could. She'd given her life serving her country since a young age and I'd read this was something she never intended since her uncle had been king until he abdicated and her father had to take over—something he never wanted. She was exactly the same age as my mother, born in 1926.

Serendipity Part One: While standing in an elevator going to breakfast, I overheard some ship officers say that Queen Elizabeth was expected at the Empress Hotel around eleven o'clock and would then give a speech on the lawn. She would fly out that afternoon on her red royal helicopter going to Vancouver to drop the ceremonial puck at the opening Canucks hockey game. Depending on any number of situations, this might delay the ship's departure and they were coming up with alternative plans. What? Seriously? The Queen would be in the same city as we were? I secretly spread the news to sixty friends and family who were traveling with us thinking we might beat the cruise passengers who rush into town. We did.

Since we arrived almost two hours before the Queen's timed appearance, we selected our place that would provide a perfect line-of-sight with no one blocking our view. We were firmly embedded, guarding our spots at the quickly-installed barrier which consisted of a rope about knee-high draped from one black and gold post to the next. Not quite the adequate security I thought for a visiting head of state. Then I remembered where we were—Canada—where people are known for being tolerant, practical, respectful and welcoming.

Serendipity Part Two: I magnanimously invited a young girl, probably about four years old, dressed in a pink satin poufy dress, to stand in front of me. You might think this kindhearted but had she been taller I wouldn't have allowed my view of impending royalty to be impaired. Her tightly curled blond hair was almost completely covered with a matching pink hat that appeared a little too big. She reminded me of a reincarnated Shirley Temple but without dimples in her smiling cheeks. Her dinky white-gloved hand was safely tucked inside her mom's who stood to my left. Her white shiny patent shoes were so clean one could almost see your reflection, and of course she wore pink floral socks. They both stood quietly and waited, almost in reverence. She securely held one long-stemmed deep pink rose in her right hand. I asked her about the rose and as she pointed across the street, said they'd just bought it at that florist shop. It was called, "The Queen of England" rose. Well, of course it was.

The seven-car motorcade pulled up and regally, almost humbly with a slight smile on her face, the real live Queen Elizabeth stepped out to shouts of welcome and clapping. She looked impeccably and elegantly dressed wearing a straight-cut, apricot-colored wool coat with matching rounded hat complete with sensible black matronly-looking pumps, obviously comfortable for lots of walking. Black gloves matched her handbag and shoes, and the trim on her coat and hat.

As she strolled down the expansive walkway to the Empress Hotel, she moved toward the crowd to greet people, mostly children. Her smile widened and she seemed to be really enjoying herself. No more than five feet in front of us walked Queen Elizabeth II, the real-life Queen Elizabeth of the British Monarchy, that each time I'd been in England I yearned to see. Then the benevolent gesture on my part turned out to be an unexpected reward for us as the Queen made a deliberate bee-line directly over to our little pink girl who was thunderstruck, as were we. The Queen smiled and said, "Is that for me?" Our little girl could only nod her head, then foisted the rose towards the Queen who graciously accepted it. Only smiling, our little girl could say nothing, but the Queen added, "Thank you for your kindness." I have been royal-struck ever since. I bought myself an English bone china tea cup and saucer set with the Queen's face proudly displayed as a lasting memento. That afternoon we listened to her speech as it was broadcast over the loud speakers. She thanked the Canadian people for their loyalty, encouragement and support during the fifty years of her reign. This would be as good as it would ever get for encountering royalty.

Later that morning, leaving promptly at eleven o'clock, we embarked on another first for our merry band of travelers. We were going to the mysterious Stonehenge via a little detour to Salisbury and stopping first at the cathedral. The peaceful drive through the countryside with hedgerows of bushes and shrubs, many blooming with unfamiliar wildflowers, became rather typical but nevertheless impressive. Soon, I could see a cathedral spire looming miles away. Tom explained it is Britain's tallest spire and its original name had been Cathedral of the Blessed Virgin Mary, Salisbury. The first cathedral had been completed at Old Sarum in 1092. Problems with the military and scarce water supplies led to an alternative location being needed and in 1220 a new site for the cathedral was at New Sarum. Then the traumas that hit England in the first half of the last century, two World Wars along with their Great Depression, meant that there were few changes to the cathedral until the gradual growth of better times and more funding dozens of years later. Worries about the stability of the structure in 1950 caused the rebuilding of the top of the spire and then in 1980, a spire fundraising appeal initiated the major restoration program.

We were fortunate to be there eleven years later and, sporting hard hats, were treated to the official tower tour, sixty feet up in the back of the cathedral. We saw the interior of the hollow spire with its ancient wood scaffolding. The cathedral also has the largest cloister and the world's oldest working clock from 1386 AD. Plus, for history's sake, it houses the best of the surviving four original copies of the Magna Carta. Our tall, dapper, white-headed, very-British-looking guide told us of the significance of this document agreed to by King John of England near Windsor in 1215. It had been drafted to make peace between the unpopular king and a group of rebel barons. It swore the safeguard of church rights, protection for the barons from illegal jail time, access to swift justice and limitations on feudal payments to the Crown, to be fulfilled through a council of twenty-five barons. However, neither side stood behind their commitments and the charter was annulled by Pope Innocent III. In 1216 and after John's death, his son, Henry III, reissued the document and stripped it of some of its more radical content. At the end of the war in 1217, it formed part of the peace treaty. There the document got the name Magna Carta and was confirmed part of England's law in 1297. Our guide explained that it had been modified over the centuries and some even tried to overturn it. He told us, for our benefit, how it influenced the early American colonists and the formation of our Constitution in 1878, which became the law of the land in the new republic of the United States. I felt embarrassed he knew more about my country's history than I did. It was indeed a most impressive cathedral with more history than the average person could retain.

Back in our motor coach the terrain flattened and we could see in the distance the mystical Stonehenge, the prehistoric standing stones, Neolithic and Bronze Age monuments in England. Nearby were several hundred burial mounds around the area that are mostly overlooked because everyone wants to see the standing rocks. Some say it was constructed over five thousand years ago. Many scholars say it could have been a burial ground from its earliest times. And of course, no one knows how or why they were really put there. For some reason, I felt unworthy walking in the footsteps of my Neolithic ancestors in one of the wonders of the world.

The stones are up to thirty feet tall and weighed twenty-five tons on average. It was speculated that they were brought from Marlborough Downs, about twenty miles north. How did they do that? The smaller stones, referred to as "bluestones," weigh only four tons, having been transported as far as one hundred forty miles from Wales—maybe. How in the world would they be able to move tons of stones without equipment? Maybe in the last ice age the glaciers carried the bluestones closer to the Stonehenge area so the monument makers didn't have to haul them all the way from Wales. And I didn't see any rivers close by to move them by raft. All speculation.

I have determined that I don't always need to know the answers to everything, and mystery every now and then is a good thing. I decided to go with the alien theory—the same aliens that abducted the Incas from Machu Picchu helped move these stones.

I'd heard about an after-dark tour through the Cotswolds so signed up those who weren't afraid of the dark the following evening. Our humorous and very knowledgeable guide, Bruce, with Lofty the bus driver, took us on what turned out to be a ghost and pub tour through the little villages and countryside.

We climbed over wooden stiles (like steps or ladders) which Bruce explained provided passage over fences and gaps. He told us stiles are often built in rural areas along footpaths, fences, walls or hedges to prevent farm animals moving from one pasture to another while enabling walkers to use the path. We traipsed through fields and around animals, mostly cows and horses, on our way to ruins and secret places. We stopped at the White Hart in Wadsworth for some Tetley Bitters and an orange Hooch for me, and Walkers Crisps. On our return trip, we visited the spooky Rollright Stones in the pitch dark. I was all for it; others, not so much. But again, no spirits, no chills or thrills, although I tried my hardest to feel something.

Peeking at my travel alarm flashing seven o'clock the next morning, I arose quietly, not to disturb my husband, but instead to surprise him in twenty minutes with coffee and a pastry. It was already one of those crystal clear sunny mornings that you knew would be a splendid start to a new day. I decided to see some different scenery on the way to the covered market. Trying a different route, I rounded a corner and to the left sat a squatty house much like I imagined a hobbit would live in. The petite garden appeared chock-full of all sizes and types of green bushes with one tiny stone bench. But what really caught my attention was an arched, hobbit-size, moss-covered old door leading somewhere. But where? I couldn't tell. On the right side of the green door bloomed one single red rose. The greenery of the rose bush blended in well with the mossy door causing the red rose to pop almost like a red ornament would on a Christmas tree. I stared at the miniature dwelling that looked out of place as it was surrounded by monumental buildings. Engrossed with my new find and clearly not paying enough attention, I glanced to the left and saw no vehicles. I stepped off the curb as I heard a brief honk and looked to the right to see a truck "lorry" hauling a load of crated chickens, barreling down towards me. I jumped back on the curb and reminded myself to look right, then left, just the opposite of what we do in America and most of Europe. Fortunately, the truck was going slowly through town so I was in no immediate peril but I reminded myself I must be better prepared for London.

That day on our way to Bath we drove through the charming south central countryside containing the Cotswolds, a range of rolling green hills which rise from the meadows of the upper Thames. Here golden Cotswold stone is quarried. The entire region is dotted with ancient, darling small townships and villages built of the Cotswold stone. The limestone is rich in fossils, particularly of fossilized sea urchins typically used in many castles and palaces like Blenheim.

Charming Castle Combe is called the prettiest village in England for good reason. It's complete with a babbling brook with white swans and a local craft market. It seemed a step-back-in-time with roofs made of split natural stone tiles. Some homes are even listed as ancient monuments. The front of a typical Cotswold home was constructed of thick stone walls. Exceptional seemed an understatement for the simply-stated St. Andrews chapel and a medieval faceless clock circa 1450. It had originally been a British hill fort occupied by the Romans, then the Normans, who built the fort up into a castle. It seemed that most homes were decorated with delicate roses climbing around doorways, with windows of lacey curtains in different patterns and window boxes overflowing with vibrant geraniums.

Twelve miles farther we were in Bath, known for its natural hot springs and 18th century Georgian buildings lining The Crescent. The historic Pulteney Bridge spans the River Avon with a wide expanse of gently cascading waterfalls called the Pulteney Weir. A weir is a barrier designed to change the river flow but nothing like a dam. This Weir was in a three-stepped horseshoe shape creating gentle, peaceful sounds of water dropping from level to level. The Weir didn't look like the waterfalls we had in Oregon, but instead, a lazy, wide, calm drop from step to step.

The original Roman Baths included the Great Bath, which were in surprisingly good condition with marble statues scattered about and an impressive temple. We chose not to soak in the waters but instead headed to The Pump Room, serving a popular afternoon tea where we tried all sorts of delectable delights. We scarfed down: crustless cucumber sandwiches (What—sandwiches without crust?), freshly baked fruit scones with clotted cream plus lemon curd, fresh fruit tarts, chocolate and coffee opera cake, raspberry choux, macaroons, a traditional Bath Bun with cinnamon butter, Pump Room poppy seed cake with lemon drizzle and Victoria Sponge served with piping hot English tea in flowery English bone china tea cups. What an indulgence! We savored every morsel. I licked the spoon after using it to scrape the last droplet of lemon curd from the petite English porcelain dish.

By now we were drinking English tea often and had been shown the proper way of preparing and serving it, well, sort of. My question, revealing my lack of British culture and protocol seemed harmless enough, "Do I put the milk (I knew not to use cream) in the bottom of the English bone china tea cup before OR after pouring in the scalding hot water?"

The instructions seemed simple:

#1. Boil freshly drawn water. Now another question: "Boil on the stove in a kettle or in the microwave?" A fine English lady looked down her narrow pointy nose through her thin half-sized reading glasses and said, "Never in a microwave, dear."

#2. Get your tea ready in the cup or mug. Again, my English instructor said, "An English bone china tea cup is always the preferred, dear." I said, "Another question, please? Tea bag or loose leaf?" She replied, "Does this really require an answer, dear?" With raised eyebrows and a sideways glance at Martha, I gently and oh so slightly tilted towards her and whispered, "I'm done with questions." Martha didn't dare reply.

#3. Pour the boiling water over the tea, stir briefly. Now here's the problem: If you're using loose leaf tea it's an entirely different process than with a tea bag. So, we're going with the tea bag instructions since that's what I'd be doing at home.

#4. Tea apparently needs time to develop its flavor. This is called steeping or brewing or drawing. Let it stand or sit for a minute or two per cup.

#5. Remove the tea. Never squeeze a tea bag, simply take it out and throw away. It will be hot and will burn your fingers.

#6. The most important part according to many: Depending on which way you brew the tea, pour the milk in before or after the hot water; the milk is important. It's all about checking for just the right color. The perfect cup will have a dark orangish-brown look. Warning: If you use tea leaves you need a strainer.

Fortified with the education on proper tea etiquette and now sustained with nourishment, we drove towards Stratford-upon-Avon. But first we stopped at Anne Hathaway's twelve-room thatched-roof cottage—typical Tudor architecture—painted white with black timber framing. It's really a farmhouse, not merely a cottage as a cottage implies small and this certainly was not. This had been the childhood home of Anne, and where William Shakespeare would have come courting, living in Stratford just one mile away. The beautiful thatched farmhouse had been occupied by descendants of the Hathaways until its purchase by the Trust in 1892. It still contained many rare family items of furniture that date back to Anne's time. The tour gave us an opportunity to explore the six-hundred-year-old house and some of the furniture including the four-poster bed and the courting settee which looked like a couch or futon. There were dazzling grounds and

gardens which overflowed with fragrant blooms of very tall hollyhocks, delphiniums and all types of dahlias and perfectly trimmed boxwood shrubs. The cottage is in Shottery, a hamlet within the parish of Stratford-upon-Avon.

We learned from the house's official guide at the cottage that eighteen-year-old William married twenty-six-year-old Anne in 1582. Six months later, Anne gave birth to their daughter, Susanna, and two years later, twins Hamnet and Judith. Sometime after the birth of their children, William set off to London's theatrical world as an actor and playwright. Anne stayed behind in Stratford with the children. There is a lot of speculation about Anne and various stories exist. Some suggest she had been a country bumpkin that he left behind. Others drew a more favorable picture, such as she was the love that inspired Shakespeare. And there is much more speculation that the guide explained but got rather confusing. Then there was the matter of William's will and more speculation. But the bottom line is that it is impossible to determine any real sense of William's relationship with Anne from the little evidence available. Mrs. Shakespeare is just one of the many mysteries of William's life. His earliest plays, including The *Comedy of Errors* and *The Taming of the Shrew*, were written in the early 1590s. Later he wrote the tragedy *Romeo and Juliet* and comedies including *The Merchant of Venice*. His most well-known tragedies were written after 1600: *Hamlet*, *King Lear*, and *Macbeth*. I recalled *Macbeth* as it had been required reading as a sophomore in high school, not one of my favorites. William became a member of the popular theater troupe "The

143

Lord Chamberlain's Men," which later became "The King's Men." This group built and operated the famous Globe Theatre in 1599. He made enough money to buy a large house in Stratford and retired in 1610, where he wrote his last plays including "*The Tempest*" and "*The Winter's Tale.*" And he had written sonnets that were published in 1609. We ducked under low ceilings touring the sparsely-appointed Shakespeare home where he lived during his childhood until he moved to London. Like Anne's farmhouse, the Shakespeare home appeared typical Tudor style. The town of Stratford-upon-Avon itself is a pleasant village with plenty of shops to buy any type of souvenir but we were really there to focus on William.

We visited Shakespeare's Church, actually the Church of the Holy Trinity sitting on the banks of the River Avon, dated from the 13th century. This was no small church and I'd classify it really as a cathedral compared to others we'd seen. It looked to be one of the prettiest churches in the world. Standing in the middle of the long stone pathway, I saw on the church, arches and carved statues along with a boxy, white and gold base that held a single protruding spire on the top. Inside were significant stained glass windows lining the top half of the walls featuring Biblical saints, with one huge window behind the alter at the front of the sanctuary. I walked up front to William's grave and there sat a red rose in a brass vase by the plaque that read, "Good friend for Jesus's sake forbear, to dig the dust enclosed here. Blessed be the man that spares these stones, and cursed be he that moves my bones."

There were three impressive manual pipe organs. We sat in silence on a wooden pew as a woman at one organ practiced for a concert that evening. The musical tones bounced off the stone walls echoing through this sacred age-old church. I felt like I could be transported to Heaven right then and there. Shakespeare returned to its peacefulness when he retired from the theater and London. I could see why.

Strolling outside, Tom mentioned that many commonly used quotes are associated with Shakespeare, such as: a foregone conclusion, a sorry sight, all of a sudden, as dead as a doornail, dash to pieces, in a pickle, primrose path, star crossed lovers, the game is up, up in arms and dozens more.

My guess is that millions of visitors from all over the world have come to see Shakespeare's monument in the chancel and his tomb in the sanctuary. Anne outlived William and had a monument erected within seven years of his death. She is buried next to her husband so one would assume they had shared some fondness for her to select her final resting place next to him.

Several years after our visit, I watched a movie called *Shakespeare in Love*, completely filmed on location. When William apparently needed some inspiration to break a bad case of writer's block, he had a secret romance with Lady Viola. His creative juices start flowing and he wrote like never before. He found out Lady Viola was successfully impersonating a man in order to play the lead in his latest production. Watching that comedy instantly took me back to standing at Anne's childhood home in Shottery and William's home in Stratford.

145

After the warm afternoon stroll from the church back into Stratford, a group of us decided we needed some libation to perk us up. We passed The Queens Head, The Rose & Crown and The Golden Bee before settling on the Dirty Duck situated on the waterside of the River Avon. I really liked these names of restaurants and pubs and asked how this pub got its name. The pub really had two names, the older being The Black Swan but the new name originated from American GIs that camped over the river in World War II.

Not being fond of ales, bitters, lager, porter or anything smelling of beer of any kind, the patient proprietor asked what types of beverages I preferred. I replied citrus and not too sweet. A bartender handed me a tall glass and bottle of Hooper's Hooch to try. This was in no way connected to our guide Tom Hooper, but I think he wished it had been for obvious monetary advantages. Shortened to Hooch, it was an alcoholic "ade" with choices of lemon, orange, lime or berry. It tasted like lemonade with a little kick, or a punch, depending on how much one drank. One seemed plenty for me and very refreshing. Over the next week, I tried each flavor, liking lemon the best.

Everyone met up at The Box Tree restaurant for dinner before the Shakespearean play. Our seats by the window provided a marvelous view of the River Avon and a low bridge with multiple arches. We watched the narrowboats navigating around and dodging the swans. Tom told us the Queen was the owner and caretaker of Britain's swans. The boats go around the swans.

We were spoiled with a delicious multi-course meal starting with Avocado Pear with Orange, served with cottage cheese and an orange dressing. The main course was Supreme of Salmon Primavera—poached salmon with white wine, served with julienne spring vegetables in a creamy saffron sauce. This came with a selection of fresh seasonal vegetables and potatoes. The crème-de-la-crème dessert was just that—the best crème brûlée I had ever tasted, maybe because it was the first I'd ever had and has caused me to be the crème brûlée snob I am today. Their specialty, Crème Brûlée Aux Cassis was delicately oven-baked with cream, egg yolks, and vanilla pods then topped with black currants and Crème de Cassis. It tasted scrumptious.

After dinner, we watched the Royal Shakespeare company present *As You Like It*. It was set in France and followed Rosalind as she escapes persecution in her uncle's court, accompanied by her cousin Celia, to find safety and eventually love in the Forest of Arden. Actors dressed as trees and bushes blended well with the actors playing live people. It is said that the quotes "All the world's a stage" and "Too much of a good thing" are from this play.

London and the Law

I had arranged for British solicitors and barristers to discuss English law with the lawyers while their families had time touring Oxford. Now it was time to get serious as we would day-trip into London for the attorneys to experience a trial in the Royal Courts of Justice, and visit the Inns of Court and the Old Bailey over the next several days.

My travelers were a punctual crew and were at the bus promptly at seven that morning. I wasn't sure if they were just polite, not wanting to make others wait, or they were afraid I would enforce the dreadful and much feared "punishment of tardiness," that being One British Pound per minute, which at that time equaled about $1.50 per minute of tardiness. The monetary threat worked the entire trip.

On our drive to London I had the microphone and was giving some instructions for the day even though we'd be met by Blue Badge Guide, Tom, and another guide, Victoria Staveley, a solicitor turned Blue Badge Guide, who would be in charge of our attorneys for the law portion of the day. While reminding them to keep their money belts tucked away, being mindful of their surroundings at all times, writing down instructions in their travel book I had provided for them including Mansfield telephone numbers and a schedule for that day, and looking to the right before stepping off into traffic, I heard a commotion in the back of the bus. Our tallest member found the bus getting a bit stuffy so he reached up to open the vent in the roof for some air.

However, it wasn't a vent but an emergency hatch on the rooftop that, when nudged, flew off, bouncing down the M40 motorway. The bus driver slammed on the brakes, expertly and carefully pulled over in rush hour traffic and scurried about one-quarter of a mile back to pick up the hatch, still in one piece but cracked. He reassured us, especially the perpetrator, that all was fine and politely explained he'd be charged for the expense if he hadn't retrieved it. The driver turned on the air conditioning for us.

We offered to pay for the damage but never saw a bill.

Our trip took slightly less than two hours even with the unexpected incident and got us into the city around nine o'clock—a city that appeared to be gridlocked in traffic. There was an unannounced strike that shut down the entire subway system called the Tube. There was much more traffic on the roadway system than normal but the locals seemed to take it in stride. We had no choice but to do the same. I could feel that familiar orbiting feeling returning.

Instead of arriving early as originally planned, thus having time to leisurely stroll around Buckingham Place—again it all looked good on paper months earlier from my office in Salem, Oregon—we went to Plan B arriving at 10:30 a.m. at a location Tom gave us. It was his insider's tip on where to meet him for the eleven o'clock Horse Guard Parade for The Changing of the Guard at Horse Guards Arch. Tom took charge and explained what we were seeing and would be viewing. It was the official main entrance of both St. James's Palace and Buckingham Palace. Bells peeled as the riders came through the arches on beautiful black horses decked out in shiny silver horse accessories. Riders on horses paraded through the yard, lined up with their silver helmets shimmering brightly and rode up the street towards the palace with one lone white horse leading the way. The Queen's Household Cavalry is the mounted guard at the entrance to Horse Guards Arch. The mounted sentries on black horses, who change every hour, are on duty each day from ten o'clock in the morning until four o'clock in the afternoon, at which time there is a dismounting parade of the Guard. The Life Guards are all dressed in red. The Blues and Royals are dressed in blue. This tradition began in the Tudor days. Seven men were dressed in white pants with black boots almost to their hips, red tunics and silver helmets with gold trim. A distinguished man dressed totally in black drew his sword, went to each Life Guard and did a ceremonial short sword display. Then he walked around behind each one, paused, like he was checking them out one final time. The Guards put their swords away, marched proudly stepping very high and departed through an arch.

Tom told us this was the best place to get up close and personal to the guards. There were two dismounted sentries on duty until the gates closed at eight o'clock when only one lone sentry was left on guard until seven the next morning. Tried as we might, they didn't crack a smile but we all got our photos with the stoic British guards dressed in red with their tall bushy, black hats.

Once we saw enough we sprinted across the lawns and streets to get to Buckingham Palace to watch the official Changing of the Guard at 11:30 a.m. in the forecourt. We listened on the way as Tom told us that the guard is usually one of the five regiments of foot guards: Grenadier Guards, Coldstream Guards, Scots Guards, Irish Guards and Welsh Guards and these men usually had served in some part of the armed forces.

He pointed out that the Queen was "home," indicated by the royal flag flying on top of the Palace and that it is the London residence and administrative headquarters of the reigning monarch. Looking at the balcony, I recalled the wedding of Diana and Charles and how they came out and waved to thousands of their subjects after their wedding.

Here's what I saw and learned from Tom: Changing of the Guard or Guard Mounting is the process of a new guard exchanging duty with the old guard. Sounds simple enough but it is anything but. The guard that looks after Buckingham Palace is called The Queen's Guard and is divided into two detachments. The Palace is responsible for guarding the palace, and the St. James Palace, responsible for guarding St. James's Palace. It is still the official center of the royal court. All the foot guards were wearing the traditional red wool tunics that looked hot and heavy, especially since it was already 25.5 degrees Celsius, or for us, 78 degrees. They also wore the very tall black bearskin hats that looked top heavy as if a light breeze could topple them easily.

The entire ceremony was set to music by a full military band of about thirty-five musicians with the entire first two rows of trombones leading the way, then trumpets, French horns, cymbals, flutes, drums, bugles, trumpets, clarinets, saxophones, more horns, and lots of precise marching. When the new guard was formed up, led by the band, it marched across into the forecourt of the palace. Once there, the new guard advanced toward the old guard in slow time, high stepping and then stopped. It was precise and I didn't see one misstep. The old guard presented arms, followed by the new guard presenting arms. The Captains of the Guard marched forward to each other for the handing over of the palace keys. The replacements were marched to the guardroom of the palaces where new sentries were now posted.

At the same time, the band moved by the center gate and formed up in a half circle, where it played music to entertain the new and old guard as well as visitors. Next, two regiment colors were paraded up and down by officers. With the old and new guards formed up, once again the old guard and the band marched through the center gates in slow time to their regimental slow march. Towards the end of the slow march, the captain of the old guard gave the word of command to "Break into Quick Time" and with a brisk five-pace roll from the drums the band led the way back to the barracks. It was British pomp and ceremony at its finest. I became a royal groupie from that day forth and quite enamored with the traditions that seemed way over-the-top but oh, so impressive.

We made it to our luncheon stop in the nick of time. I'd made reservations for our group at the legendary lawyers' and journalists' hangout, The Wig and Pen Club, at 229-230 Strand. The first floor held the main bar area which had been the London Press Club members' bar. We ate our lunch in The Cell and I pondered, if these walls could talk, what secrets they would divulge. I had the Sir Walter Raleigh chicken but it wasn't really the chicken dish that appealed to me—it was the name. Hundreds of famous people had sat right here just like me. The Club had been built on Roman ruins in 1624 and was said to be the only structure on the Strand to have survived the Great Fire of London in 1666. The

Royal Courts of Justice were close by where our attorneys would be spending some time learning English law.

That afternoon, we were greeted at The Tower of London by the Beefeaters, dressed in wool, even in the summer, with boxy navy-with-red-trimmed hats and red-collared, knee-length coats and slacks. The red trim stood out on the plain navy along with the large letters "ER" (for Elizabeth Regina) on the chest just below the royal crown insignia. And they wore very shiny black shoes.

The Tower is where the nation's crown jewels are displayed. As we rode the flat people-mover by the gleaming Imperial State Crown, I wondered how anyone could balance it on one's head. White fur lined the bottom with every jewel imaginable in different colors and shapes. It must have weighed twenty pounds. St. Edward's crown from 1661 looked just as impressive and even larger—my guess, about twenty-five pounds of gold and jewels. There was a wine cistern, or to me the grand punch bowl from 1829, bejeweled scepters, spears and much more. At the medieval White Tower, we visited the royal apartments of King Edward I. On the way, we saw the Yeoman Warders and period costumes showing life in the 13th century royal court.

The White Tower had been built in 1078 by William the Conqueror. It was the start of the Tower of London's history as a palace and fortress. It contained lots of armor and weapons, not my cup of tea but there was an impressive British carriage from 1827 complete with a Flemish bronze gun from 1607 and a full-size lion at the back. The wall walk allowed us to stroll along the battlements of the Tower's inner wall. King Henry III built the wall in the 13th century to protect the White Tower. As we looked over the wall to where it had once been connected to the river, the BBC cameras and people were filming but I didn't spot any familiar actors or royalty. The Cradle Tower tells the story of one of the few successful attempts to escape from the Tower of London. Beauchamp Tower, where many prisoners were held, still has eerie inscriptions etched on the walls. Ravens are a big deal here and have lived in the Tower since its beginnings. They even had their own lodgings. In the 17th century King Charles II decreed that six ravens should be kept there permanently. We saw several of them protecting their turf and we were careful not to try to pet them as Tom warned us they do bite. We didn't make it into each tower and site but we did stop at the gift shop with faux jeweled crowns and jewelry, rubber weapons and metal letter opener in the shape of a sword which one person in our group found out did not make it home in carry-on luggage.

The next day we left again for our two-hour bus ride to London and arrived earlier than anticipated. The Tube strike was over. We were dressed up in professional attire as all of us would have a special day being a part of English protocol and law. While waiting to be escorted into a private room for a reception at The Honourable Society of the Middle Temple, commonly known as Middle Temple, our very distinguished elderly guide showed us around. He proudly proclaimed it was the finest example of an Elizabethan Hall in London. At one-hundred-one-feet-long and forty-one feet wide, it is spanned by a

magnificent double hammerbeam roof. Begun in
1562, it has changed little to the present day. He said
that Middle Temple is one of the four Inns of Court
exclusively entitled to call their members to the
English Bar as barristers, the others being the Temple
Inn, Gray's Inn and Lincoln's Inn. It is located near
the Royal Courts of Justice. The High Table is a four-
hundred-year-old wood table that consists of three
twenty-nine-foot planks of single oak, a gift from
Elizabeth I to Middle Temple, cut down in Windsor
Forest and floated down the Thames to be installed
in Middle Temple Hall before the building had even
been completed. Our host continued saying that The
Benchers of the Inn (masters of the bench or senior
members) today still dine as they did that evening in
August 1586 when Francis Drake, just back from a
successful expedition against the Spanish Indies, was
congratulated by Benchers and members. According
to tradition, the hatch of his ship, the Golden Hind,
was later used to make the present "cupboard," a
table which stands below the Bench table. We heard
a lot about the significance of this stunning building;
however, it was not just a historic relic, it is the center
of the life of the Inn today. Bench, bar and students
meet here daily at lunch and the evenings during
dining times.

In Middle Temple we were treated to a sherry
reception in the dining room before having a
prestigious lunch at High Table Middle Temple Hall.
We were formally escorted in and the sight took my
breath away. There were four long rows with tables
set for eight, lined end to end with a buffet set up on
the left. There were two more special tables going the
opposite direction to the others, where some judges

sat. We were taken down the far right aisle and seated at High Table, a step above everyone else. We all stood at attention until we were told to be seated. The linens, china and cutlery were perfectly set. We were seated under six substantial oil portraits of several queens and kings. I had the distinct feeling of being looked down on, with them probably curious why Americans were sitting at their High Table.

The first course was Stilton Mousse and Poached Pear followed by Salmon Hollandaise, Jersey New Potatoes, mangetouts (snap peas), topped off by a dessert of Summer Pudding stuffed with blueberries and blackberries, complete with Middle Temple White and Red Wine. We were there on the Fourth of July. It seemed fitting somehow.

To get some idea of how special it was to be at High Table one must study English Law. Let me just say, we were actually elevated on a step above all the other barristers, solicitors plus judges, who frequented Middle Temple on a regular basis. Our extraordinary Blue Badge Guide, Tom, had been a barrister for over twenty years before retiring from the law. As a barrister and member of Middle Temple, he'd eaten hundreds of meals there but he had never been invited to High Table, ever. He felt quite honored to finally arrive...even though via the Americans. He asked how I had accomplished such a feat because sitting at the distinguished High Table was almost unheard of, especially for a group of Americans. I politely declined sharing my state secrets; some, I replied, should stay just that—a secret.

Following lunch we visited the Norman Temple Church, built in 1185, a perfectly round church belonging to the Inn and Middle Temples. The Norman church had magnificent stained glass and hundreds of gargoyles adorning the round church aisle arcade. One gargoyle grimaced in pain as a dog appeared to bite his ear. Of course, there must have been some explanation for that but I never heard it. I found no smiling gargoyles. Next we went for a tour of the City of London Law Society, one of the largest law societies in the United Kingdom. And tea, of course. It seemed everything revolved around tea with milk and sugar. Trying to duplicate English tea at home would not be the same.

After our two-hour ride in our comfortable Pearce's motor coach we were back for the evening at Mansfield. That night in honor of our Independence Day, they decorated with an American Flag and their British Flag but there were some humorous remarks about us leaving the homeland hundreds of years earlier and the British never being quite the same again. We felt honored that Principal Trevaylean and his wife, Carol, joined us.

The menu that night, their version of High Table, was: Melon Fan with Wildberry Confit, Mushroom á la Crème, then Moules Bonne Femme, a main course of Escalopes of Turkey with Tomato and Thyme, Brie and Spinach Parcels, new potatoes, mangetouts, sautéed courgettes (zucchini) topped off with Crêpes Grand Marnier for dessert. Whoever said that British food tasted blah and bland hadn't been there in a while. They served us their special stock of Mansfield wines, Plovdiv Cabernet Sauvignon 1991 and Calvet Blanc. We felt like royalty. And whoever gets two High Tables in one day? We topped off the evening with a party in the Old Bar at Mansfield, drinking some local beverages and toasting our Fourth of July. No fireworks were needed. This day had been memorable enough.

The following day we returned to London and visited Westminster Abbey. My guess is The Abbey, nestled in the heart of London, is the most photographed building in London. It seems whenever there was news from London, the reporter was standing at the Abbey. It was a place of incredible beauty, a place of worship, weddings and funerals—a church whose life has been closely identified with Great Britain for more than nine hundred years. Tom guided us solemnly through as I walked gingerly on the black and white square-tiled floor; I felt like I might be intruding on hallowed ground and it was highly likely somebody had been buried below. In the Abbey was the Musicians' Aisle—graves and memorials of famous musicians, including three of the greatest organists of the Abbey. The Statesmen's Aisle contains graves and memorials of many famous British statesmen including Prime Ministers Disraeli and Gladstone. The Lantern, where the fun happens, coronations and royal weddings took place at the High Altar. Remembering to gaze upwards I saw the magnificent vaulted roof, begun in the 13th century and completed soon after 1500. Until the middle of the 16th century the Abbey had been a Benedictine monastery and the monks sang their daily services in the enclosed choir. Now, visitors are welcome to share in the worship. Then there was the tomb of Queen Elizabeth I who was buried with her half-sister, Queen Mary Tudor, in an ornate display.

The Chapel of King Henry VII showed off the walls of the Knights, whose banners hang above them plus several kings and queens. Considered the most sacred place in the Abbey is the Chapel of St. Edward the Confessor. He was a Saxon King (1042-1066) and the founder of the Abbey. Tom continued his narration explaining that these royal tombs held something very controversial. The Coronation Chair had been made for Edward I and enclosed the Stone of Scone on which Scottish kings were crowned. It had been taken to England in 1296. Tom said the Scottish weren't happy about it at all and regularly demanded it be returned to its rightful country. I got the impression the English wanted the Scottish to think they were one big happy family under the big cap called Great Britain. It didn't seem like the Scottish were buying into it.

We saw the Tomb of Mary, Queen of Scots, who was gruesomely beheaded in 1587. Nearby is the exquisite tomb of Lady Beaufort, mother of Henry VII, and before the altar is the burial place of Queen Anne, King Charles II, King William III and Queen Mary II. All of these queens and kings reminded me again how we are such a young country with no royalty. One could go either way on the pros and cons of this topic. The Poet's Corner is the final resting place for major English poets and some writers such as Charles Dickens, Dylan Thomas, Geoffrey Chaucer, T.S. Eliot. The Nave, just inside the Great West Door was a memorial to Winston Churchill and nearby is the grave of the Unknown Warrior, commemorating those who were killed in the Great War 1914-1918. I noticed Franklin D. Roosevelt had a memorial here.

Even though the Abbey is a memorial for many historical figures, worship remains the primary function. Local Londoners and some visitors were using the two prayer chapels. I felt refreshed and renewed and inspired to return one day. I have said that now for a total of seven times. Writing this story, some twenty years after the first visit, I realize that I never tire spending time in this glorious place of worship.

As we walked by the Parliament buildings, we heard the four-faced, chiming clock Big Ben, playing some tune. We toured the Cabinet War Rooms, which had recently opened for touring. This served as Churchill's headquarters during World War II. It was an excellent re-creation of living underground with his staff and various electronics including over a dozen colored telephones—one red, two solid green and most white except for two black phones with green receivers. They each had a different significance. The underground bunker revealed the secrets and espionage that went on below ground during the war. And we saw where the prime minister slept in sparse quarters with the wall of his bedroom covered by a huge world map.

That afternoon, while the attorneys were observing a trial at the Old Bailey, we toured another recognizable sight in London—St. Paul's Cathedral—an Anglican church built in English Baroque style. The architect was Sir Christopher Wren. We had already seen several of the masterpieces he worked on. Calling it an impressive building seemed like an understatement with the dome framed by the two spires, and until 1962, had been the tallest building in London.

The Whispering Gallery is a circular gallery in the Cathedral that runs at the point where the vault of the dome starts to curve inwards. The name comes from the fact that a person who whispers facing the wall on one side can be clearly heard on the other, since the sound is carried perfectly around the dome. Of course, we had to test it. I stood facing the wall talking and Tom positioned himself on the other side as he repeated to the group what I was whispering, "Four score and seven years ago our fathers brought forth on this continent a new nation, conceived in liberty, and dedicated to the proposition that all men are created equal." We proved The Whispering Gallery true and I knew Tom would appreciate the first line from President Lincoln's Gettysburg Address.

I remembered seeing an incredible photo from World War II of the image of the dome surrounded by the smoke and fire of the Blitz. The cathedral had been used for funerals of Lord Nelson, the Duke of Wellington and Sir Winston Churchill, jubilee celebrations for Queen Victoria, and peace services marking the end of the First and Second World Wars. But what I knew mostly about the cathedral had been the wedding of the naïve and unprepared, in my opinion, Diana Spencer who married Prince Charles, fifteen years earlier. From my admittedly limited reading and television coverage, I still concluded I didn't like Prince Charles at all. They were divorced in 1996, the same year we were visiting, and it seemed clear to me it had been completely his fault.

The English people I met were huge fans of Diana and referred to her as the Peoples' Princess. They appreciated that she seemed more like an everyday person than the rigid, out-of-date royal family. She had been involved with dozens of charities. It appeared she took an active role in her sons' lives. Most seemed disappointed and annoyed with the royal family because of the way Diana had been treated by them. And it made it worse that she had no privacy from the photographers and tabloids.

I seemed a bit more interested in this miserable, heart-wrenching saga than the rest of our group. I had stayed up all night and early morning on July 29, 1981, watching the British spectacle-of-a-wedding live on television. It looked magnificent, splendid, grand, stunning and the English knew how to put on a show. Diana was the Princess of Wales, her middle name was Frances, same as mine. Her initials were DFW, for Diana Frances Windsor—Windsor being the official last name by marriage. We shared the exact same initials, just different first and last names. I thought a few times about writing her to explain our commonality in names but my good sense got the better of me. And, I was still on full royal alert hoping to spot Diana or the Queen.

We walked by a tribute to William Wallace which read, "To the immortal memory of Sir William Wallace, Scottish Patriot, born at Elderslie Renfrewshire circa 1270 AD, who from the year 1296 fought dauntlessly in defence of his country's liberty and independence in the face of fearful odds and great hardship being eventually betrayed and captured. Brought to London and put to death near

162

this spot on the 23rd August 1305. His example of heroism and devotion inspired those who came after him to win victory from defeat and his memory remains for all time a source of pride, honour and inspiration to his countrymen." I'd heard family lore that my mother's family were descendants of Wallace. I would be exploring that in the near future.

Next, Tom showed us an open area displaying the old city ruins which were on the way to The Priory Church of St. Bartholomew-The-Great, or to locals, Great St. Bart's. It's hidden and tucked in so you must actually know where you're going to find them. The oriel window allegedly had been built so Prior Bolton could keep an eye on the monks. It became my favorite church in London with the arches, naves, chapels, wooden-beamed ceiling and sunbeams streaming in the windows. The church hosted many executions particularly during the reign of Mary Tudor. There was a ghost fabled to haunt the church and there had been several reports of an elderly lady who had been sighted walking in the church after hours, accompanied by a strong smell of floral perfume. Then she disappeared, leaving witnesses with a sense of foreboding doom. Fortunately, or unfortunately, we didn't encounter any apparition.

Late that afternoon we were strolling along the Thames wasting time before going to Her Majesty's Theatre for the performance of *Phantom of the Opera*, where we saw our first sighting of black swans. Their bright red bills seemed to disappear into the black feathers on their heads. Two began to intertwine necks and went through some sort of lovely ritual. Maybe this is where the term "necking" started. The Brits did like to take credit for most original sayings and slogans.

We saw the Elizabethan playhouse, Shakespeare's Globe Theatre, originally built in 1599, then destroyed by fire, rebuilt and then demolished. The new Globe Theatre hopefully would be open the following summer and we were told it would look much like the original, as much as they could tell from old photos and historic information. The play, *Henry V*, would be the opening production.

Zipping to and fro were compact cars called Smart Cars. Even though these cars are two-seaters, I felt certain most Americans would have a difficult time squeezing in, especially two. But two of these cars would fit easily into one of our parking spaces at home. Tom explained that the brand name stemmed from Swatch (the watch makers) and Mercedes in the early 1980s when the CEO developed an idea for a new car using the same type of manufacturing tactics and personalized features used to popularize Swatch watches. He thought the auto industry had overlooked potential customers who wanted a small, yet stylish city car. We saw Smart Cars painted with blazing solid neon colors and some with solid humdrum hues and some dazzling ones with flamboyant orange flames, black and white checkerboard, one painted like a tank, one with a top hat on the roof, a black one with a lightning bolt, a rainbow, the sun in a variety of looks, countless two-toned, and oodles of cleverly and uniquely decorated three-toned. It's not as easy as one might think to pick one up.

It was almost show time as we entered Her Majesty's Theatre in the West End. We learned that the name of the theater changes with the sex of the monarch. It became Her Majesty's Theatre when Elizabeth became queen. Walking in, I saw a Corinthian colonnade rising to the second floor forming a loggia in front of the circle foyer. This was hovering above a canopy over the main ground floor entrances. Everywhere I looked I saw gleaming, opulent, immense architecture. We took our seats and as the haunting music started playing, louder and louder, I became entranced by it and the detailed scenery on the stage. When the phantom kidnapped Christine—seriously…how did they cause the boat to appear as if it was floating on the nonexistent water? And how did they get the phantom to fly across the auditorium without any wires or lines showing? I bought a CD as a memento of the extra-ordinary theatrical performance that I couldn't wait to see again one day.

On our final day in London we drove around the circle of the bustling Trafalgar Square. We hopped off the bus into the big public square that commemorates the Battle of Trafalgar, a naval victory in the Napoleonic Wars. Here Nelson's Column is flanked and guarded by stone lions that are worth the climb, plus everybody does it. They share the square with hundreds of pesky pigeons. The British Museum, founded in 1753, has a remarkable collection of over eight million items dedicated to human history, art and culture. Many of the exhibits were free and I concluded one could spend a few days in this museum alone; the two hours didn't do it justice.

Covent Garden wasn't far from the British Museum and I granted everyone time to wander through this former fruit and vegetable market, now a very popular shopping and tourist site. This would be the last chance for shopping and I had some serious souvenir bargain hunters. We peered down on street performers below juggling flaming bowling pins in the air. They started with four, then five, six and ended by tossing eight back and forth between the two of them. I held my breath when they hurled them higher and higher and they never dropped one. The Garden was packed with cafés, pubs, small shops and a craft market, called the Apple Market, along with another market located in the Jubilee Hall. Feeling ready for a break, we munched on chips (our French fries) sprinkled generously with malt vinegar, a sandwich of brie and avocado on crunchy-on-the-outside, soft-and-flavorful-inside French bread. And for dessert I had my favorite, crème brûlée.

After lunch we strolled past Chanel, Dior, Benjamin Pollock's Toy Shop with handmade toys of all kinds, books, puppets and music boxes, and Crabtree & Evelyn with their fine foods, gorgeous gifts and original perfumes. We had our pick of clothing and shoe stores, candy, stationery, cookies, jewelry, watches, handbags, art, sunglasses and paper products—a treat for the eyes but not the pocketbooks as the exchange rate had not been in our favor. But we did our share to support their local economy. I needed some postcards to mail home and bought the typical ones with multiple photos per card. But another one caught my attention—the same illustration appeared in four quadrants—a patch of green grass with a tree and a caricature clothed in a yellow slicker stood holding a brown umbrella in the pouring rain, called "The Four Changing Seasons of Britain." The only thing that changed in the four photos was the tree. The spring quadrant showed the tree with a few budding leaves. Summer it was fully engulfed with leaves. Autumn revealed leaves on the ground and for winter, the tree was totally bare. I chuckled because we could use the exact same card at home changing the word Britain to Oregon. I felt at home in England.

We all knew that evening would be our final one at Mansfield College. Sitting around the quad in the warmth of the summer evening we recapped the entertaining, enlightening, educational time, grateful for the opportunity to explore and meet new friends. Some asked when the next program would be. We laughed at our escapades of punting, the perfect timing of seeing Nelson Mandela, Prince Charles and the Spare of Marlborough, studying English law and the privilege of High Table at Middle Temple and touring monumental buildings and historic monuments. I felt grateful for all these first-time experiences, plus I'd acquired thirty-six new seasoned travelers, some who continue to explore new places with me to this day.

Everyday coming and going through the walnut colored dorm room door led to eventful, unique exploration and revealed history of my British heritage, even though not as much as my Scottish and Irish lineage. I blinked back tears on our final morning when I closed the walnut door to our temporary home. I felt so grateful I had the opportunity to live at Mansfield College, Oxford University, Great Britain, that first year. As it turned out, I returned twice introducing different guests, and some repeaters, to similar experiences at Oxford. Each time I entered "my" walnut door, I felt like I had returned home.

Trip Tips:

Don't forget items in your carry-on for your long flight like earplugs or noise cancelling headphones, inflatable pillow, shawl or large scarf works well as a blanket or tent to block out light, eye mask, sanitizing wipes, compression socks, sleep aids, food and water, pen and paper, chewing gum and one set of extra clothing. And don't forget your prescription medications.

Don't forget your passport and make a copy to put somewhere else in your luggage. Make a copy to leave at home with a trusted friend or relative.

Don't forget a money belt to keep your passport, credit card and large bills safely tucked away. If you have a safe in your room, lock away your passport and extra cash you don't need that day. Try to determine ahead of time how much you will need for the day. Pickpockets live all over the world and are just waiting for naïve tourists looking around at sights and not paying attention to what is happening to them.

Don't forget good walking shoes for meandering out to castle ruins or uneven cobblestone walkways.

Don't forget a rain poncho for any time of year; forget an umbrella and don't complain about the quick-changing weather.

Don't forget they drink their beer room temperature.

Don't forget there are separate taps at a sink, one for hot water and the other cold.

Don't get hit by a car or bus. Like the rest of the United Kingdom, they drive on the opposite side of the street than many other countries. Look right, left and right again before stepping out in the street.

Don't get impatient; this is a country of people who are used to queues (lining up and waiting).

British words that are helpful:

First floor means the ground floor.
Loo means toilet.
Lift means elevator.
Lounge means living room.
Underground means the subway.
Mad means crazy.
Angry means mad.
Cheers still for toasting but also used as thanks.
Scrummy means truly delicious.
Brilliant means exciting or wonderful.
Shop means little store.
Timetable means schedule.
Fortnight means two weeks.
Nappy means a diaper.
Pram means a stroller.
Sideboards means sideburns.
Chemist means a pharmacist.

Football means soccer. There is no word for
American football.
Pub means bar.
Refectory or canteen means a cafeteria.
Jacket potato means baked potato.
Minced beef means ground beef.
Chips means French fries.
Crisps means chips.
Pudding means any kind of dessert.
Sultanas means raisins.
Wardrobe means closet.
Vest means undershirt.
Jumper means sweater.
Waistcoat means vest.
Mac or mackintosh means a raincoat.
Trousers means pants.
Trainers means sneakers.
Snooker is similar to billiards or pool.
Queue means a line.
Torch means flashlight.
Mobile means cell phone.
Parcel means a package.
Holiday means vacation.
Caravan means a motor home or trailer.
Sitting on a tailback means stuck in traffic.
Bonnet means hood of car.
Boot means trunk of the car.
Car park means parking lot.
Garage can also mean a gas station.
Silencer means a muffler.
Petrol means gas.
Parkway means something you drive on.
Driveway means something you park on.

Helpful lessons I've gleaned from tour guides, travelers, blogs, books and travel articles—

Attitude: Travel with an open mind and heart. You are in a different country to see and do new things, not the same things you'd do at home. Go with an open mind of learning and don't expect England to be like America. You are invading their country, roadways, stores and restaurants. Every year, millions of tourists visit England. It's a small country, about the same square miles as Louisiana. But England has fifty-three million residents and Louisiana has over four million. The English are courteous and hospitable and can be somewhat reserved. Do not be demanding but be gracious and respectful as American superiority will not serve you well. This holds true anywhere you travel.

Overnight flights are best usually with one, maybe two, connections. Try to sleep on the plane even if you need to take something to help. When taking an overnight flight, you will land in the morning and likely arrive before you can get into your hotel room. Your room will probably not be available until mid-afternoon. So clean up a bit and maybe even change clothes at the airport or on the plane before you land. If you are renting a car at the airport and heading directly to the countryside, you can store your bags in the boot (trunk) of your car until you can check in to your room at your destination. But if you are heading directly to London from the airport, make arrangements in advance to store your bags at the hotel until your room is ready. Our jet lag prevention is to plan a low-key activity for the morning and early afternoon. This is a great time to do what we always

171

do on our first day—take the Hop On/Hop Off bus tour. And remember, when your room is ready, do not nap! Stay upright and active. Have an early, light dinner, not much alcohol and go to bed early. It works every time for us.

In London, walk or ride buses to see everything. Use the subway (The Tube) for quick transportation but avoid it at rush hour. Stand on the right side of the Tube escalators, walk on the left. A London A-Z street plan book is an invaluable resource. Local bookstores are usually a surprising and marvelous place to explore and a splendid source for all activities and local history books. If traveling by train, save money by purchasing a Railpass. Travel outside of rush hours to avoid crowds and save even more. All of this could change by the time you get there.

Don't show up without a reservation during high season. It's a very popular country and very crowded in the summer. Consider going in spring or fall where you will find less expensive accommodations, more choices and cheaper airfare. If you are thinking about summer, plan eight to nine months out for hotels and even further for bed and breakfasts as they have fewer rooms. We purchase our airline ticket as far out as possible for best pricing and look at airlines with only one stop. Also check out cheaper days to fly; Sunday seems to be most expensive.

Try out Bed and Breakfasts to get to know local people who might become friends for life. B&B's are clean, comfortable, convenient and cost less.

Warning: Some bedrooms will be a double or twin beds; ask ahead of time. Don't ever assume there is a queen or king bed anywhere. Ask about en-suite, which means a bathroom attached, but don't be surprised if you are sharing a bathroom with housemates. It can be a delightful way to interact and meet new friends instead of staying in American-style hotels.

Don't expect low-cost motels in England. B&Bs and hotels are always "double rooms" which means they have one double bed and the rate is per person (not per room) for two people sharing the room. Proprietors are often unwilling to let one person occupy a double room unless you are paying the double rate. If you are sleeping alone, you will pay more. If you want a room with two beds you must request a "twin room."

Then there's the bathrooms. Many are puzzled by British plumbing. Prepare yourself because most places have bathtubs not showers. You may have a choice but don't count on it. If you are not a bath person, you may want to pack one of those contraptions that you attach to the faucet to create your own shower. If you simply must use a shower, you will find that most are electric and the water is heated on demand, so you have to turn it on by finding a switch. If an en-suite room is available, be prepared to pay extra, but it might be worth it for you. But know that if it's en-suite, usually the room is smaller because they had to build it in so the toilet will probably be in a dinky room. Also, it is commonplace that the toilet and sink are in one room and bathtub is in another. If you ask for the

173

"bathroom" you will be shown to a room with a bathtub and no toilet. Ask for the toilet or loo if that's what you need.

Remember, too, that a B&B is not like a hotel where you can order room service. You are staying in the home that the hosts most likely live in. There are probably only one or two people available to care for all the guests, so don't ask for things like you might in a hotel. There will be specific times for breakfast, and if you are fortunate maybe delectable delights at 4 p.m., and you may need to be back by a certain time at night. The trade-off is a unique room and a reasonable price.

If you have not prebooked accommodations, ask to see a room before you decide to take it; don't stay if it doesn't work for you and don't feel like you are offending someone if you don't take it. If you pay a booking fee to a tourist board for a room, be sure to deduct it from what you owe the establishment because some places forget to take it off.

Don't go to England and just stay in London. There is much more to this marvelous country than this fabulous, traffic-filled big city. Yes, London is packed with one-of-kind British monuments, museums and churches but it is also just another big city. If you don't get out, you will miss quaint villages and beautiful countryside. Did you watch *Poldark* on PBS filmed in the Cornwall region? Or *Doc Martin* filmed in the same area? Rent a car, be bold and learn to drive on the opposite side of the road. But England is bigger than you imagine. Don't assume looking at a map really tells you the whole travel story. There is a lot of traffic and it takes longer to drive everywhere

174

including those one-lane roads that are winding and narrow. Be careful brushing up against the hedgerows when you see the lorry (truck) barreling towards you. Maybe you are nervous about driving on the other side of the road but usually in about fifteen or twenty minutes, you'll adjust. But don't even think about driving in London; rent a car when you leave.

Don't try to do too much and get stressed. Don't stay in London the entire time, and take day-trips. Lodging in London can be ridiculously expensive and even the cheapest hotels that you wouldn't want your dog to stay in can be $200 per night. Consider staying a little farther out but close to the underground station. Remember, if you are on the first floor, you will be climbing one flight of stairs; the ground floor is on the ground level. Be reasonable in your sightseeing expectations and plan to return another time to see more of this unique country.

Use the experts and take guided tours especially if it's your first visit. You will learn and hear more. Only use Blue Badge Guides. They are the most educated and knowledgeable. Guide books are great, especially for planning your trip, but you don't want to wander around missing the sights with your nose stuck in the guide book and really looking like a tourist. Or download a podcast and plug in your earbuds but keep your head and eyes upward and paying attention. When visiting some cathedrals, there may not be an admission charge. But you will see a box or container for a donation. Be generous as it costs enormous amounts of money to keep these ancient spaces open for you to enjoy and to keep them structurally sound. Show your appreciation with a big-hearted contribution.

Food is more expensive and can cost about one-third more. Staying at a B&B will give you a great start for your day, so eat a good and plentiful breakfast of protein, fruits and vegetables and try the full English breakfast. Coffee drinkers will be thrilled to know that the English know how to make really good coffee and many places serve it in French press pots. Learn how to work one before you go (check out YouTube). But drink the tea, English-style, because you can't replicate it at home.

At lunch, you can save some pound sterling and get something from a food vender or a cheap meal at a pub. Check out your guide books for cheap eats or ask locals. Our favorite sandwich of brie and avocado on crunchy bread while sitting along the banks of a river is dreamy. Most sandwiches are made with butter not mayo. A salad means something different, too. At lunch, what you think of as a "shrimp salad" sandwich is called "prawn mayonnaise." Anything "salad" (tuna salad, ham salad, chicken salad) means the item with a tossed green salad next to it. So for a "ham salad" you will receive slices of ham and a tossed green salad. Prepacked sandwiches are a favorite in the UK and found everywhere, not just convenience stores, but newspaper stands and pharmacies.

There was an old myth that English food was boring and tasteless. That is not true. They have discovered how to use fresh local produce and meats and dairy products, prepared in fresh, unique ways. Some of the best cheeses are from England, especially the rugged Cheddar Gorge area. If you get there, do your own cheese taste test and for an extra thrill, explore the caves. London is a hub of international restaurants and most towns have a variety, too. Despite what you have heard in the past, you won't have to subsist on bland, overcooked meat and potatoes. You can also find light, fresh tasty meals. Just ask a local where the best fish and chips are—greasy and probably wrapped in brown paper. Try some traditional foods and beverages in the local pubs. Pub food is always a bargain, hot and plentiful with lots of deep fried items. Check the times they are open because they are only open certain hours during the day. Pubs are known as bars but you will see entire families of all ages eating reasonably priced food. If you are in a museum or cathedral they will most likely have a "refectory" which is a cafeteria and usually a good deal and many times items will be homemade, especially desserts. Remember, they drink beer at room temperature. And water without ice. Most carbonated drinks come directly from the refrigerator and are cold enough. If you'd like ice, you should ask for it.

Expect the unexpected for weather, even in the summer. Remember, you are on an island that's in an ocean. Plan on a wide variety of temperatures even in summer and count on muggy and uncomfortably hot in London. In the countryside, it might be pleasant but expect at least a day or two of cooler weather and probably rain. If it doesn't happen, then how lucky are you? Pack accordingly and dress in layers so that you can add or subtract as needed. Take a foldable windbreaker that won't take up much room or a disposable poncho.

Your money may go further now than years gone by. Credit cards are not quite as universally accepted as in the U.S., especially by small shops. Cash is king and you will need to pay cash normally for a B&B. You can usually use your ATM card to get cash as you go but check your bank fees before departing. It is possible you won't be able to find an ATM machine or the only one you can find is out of service in some pintsize village. And don't even think about trying to exchange U.S. dollars in restaurants and stores—the conversion fees are outrageous and their calculations will vary, helping only the establishment, not you.

If you are planning to visit lots of cathedrals, museums and castles, check out the Great British Heritage Pass. The initial cost may seem a bit high but you will soon see that it pays for itself if you visit any national trust or English heritage sites. And since most of the country's main attractions are covered, you will be also.

Cars seldom stop for pedestrians—cross any street at your own risk. Sometimes there are buttons you can push for the light to turn red so you can cross a major street or highway. Don't count on the cars stopping.

Even though Britain is an English-speaking country, things can be different than they are at home.

Visit the villages and roam the countryside and most importantly, enjoy the people who live there.

"Travel opens your eyes and your heart."

Deleen Wills

The Blue and White Door

Autumn 1962 B.C. (Before Cuba)

Third grade began just like the past two school years,
Tuesday after Labor Day. I felt both anxious and
happy to be back with all my school chums after a
summer of playing around my neighborhood, and
several camping trips at the Oregon coast and
Metolius River in central Oregon with family and
friends. This summer I'd only broken one of the
neighbor's windows while playing softball in our
front yard—better than the year before. My favorite
(and extremely tolerant) neighbors, Russ and Millie,
lived right across the street and received the brunt of
many fly balls even though Russ was always the
pitcher. They were ancient, at least fifty years old. I'd
directed the younger neighborhood kids in an
outdoor play for their parents, complete with puppets, guitar, drums made from oatmeal containers
and a coronet, and sold lemonade making some
spending money. Standing beside my desk with my
hand over my heart, I recited "The Pledge of Allegiance." We did this every school day. But something
felt weird. Our normally outgoing, friendly teachers
seemed quiet.

That unexplainable feeling at school those first
few weeks stopped on Friday, October 12, 1962,
Columbus Day, when the entire Pacific Northwest
got hit by a storm named "Freda," also called the
"Big Blow." But for all of us who lived through it,
we simply called it "The Columbus Day Storm." Dad
read from the *Albany Democrat-Herald*, our local
and only newspaper, that the storm, really an

179

extratropical cyclone, was one of the most powerful recorded in the U.S. in the 20th century. It blew across southwest British Columbia, Washington, Oregon and northern California. Forty-six people died because of this storm. When our soft, black wavy-haired dog, Cappy, had died a few months earlier it felt like my heart broke in half. I cried a lot. I felt sad for the people who died in the storm.

We lived in the Willamette Valley in Oregon. Reports said that "a home that wasn't damaged was the exception." Our two-bedroom home stood in the south part of Albany, built in the middle of Hackleman's Oak Grove. Anyone growing up in our neighborhood knew the story about a farmer from Iowa named Abner Hackleman who came to Oregon in 1845 by crossing the plains with his team of oxen. He staked his claim but only stayed one year before returning home by packhorse to get his family. He died before returning. A few years later his son, Abram, located his father's claim, married a local girl and built a two-story house in the oak grove—now our oak grove. Over one hundred years later that old house sat empty down the street and around the corner and was surrounded and hidden by giant creaky old oaks. It was haunted; all of us kids knew it. Never once did I go up to that house, nor ever thought about trying to break in. A really neat thing was that Abram's great-great granddaughter Kathy attended the same church we did.

During the storm, Mom sat me and my five-year-old brother in Dad's naugahyde vinyl brown recliner far away from the large front room window. She covered us in a fort of blankets and we hid eating a bowl of candy corn that she had stocked up for Halloween. Each time a mighty oak snapped, it sounded like a gigantic toothpick being broken in half. It was an awful, thunderous and sickening noise. Mom would say, "There goes another one," as it hit the ground so hard it shook our entire house. The top-heavy trees were still loaded with colorful fall leaves. The howling winds continued without slowing down and about two hours into the storm an oak tree fell across our garage taking out power for one week. Russ and Millie joined us as they watched three trees fall surrounding their new Volvo. Russ cared more for the new car than their house where one tree had fallen on a corner of the roof.

Mom cooked our meals in the fireplace while warming baby food in a pot of boiling water for my eight-month-old baby brother. We lost over half of our stately oak trees that provided natural air conditioning in the warm summer months. I was so relieved that one of my favorite trees still stood, the one that the hoot owl family lived in it. I loved listening to them hoot to each other when we took evening strolls around our neighborhood. On some streets, entire rows of maples, elms, walnut and cherry trees were damaged, most completely uprooted or snapped off. Every neighbor got hit in some way. We missed school for a week. Mom and Dad cleaned up along with parents of my friends who had their own messes to take care of but everyone helped each other. Once all the power and telephone lines were lifted off the ground, we were allowed to finally go outside. I played with the twins, Janet and my best friend Janelle, climbing on fallen trees before they were cut up for firewood. One tree had a large limb stretched out over the neighbor's yard. It looked like a big cannon on a ship and we created our own version of Peter Pan.

Returning to school, things seemed different. We all talked about the wind storm and what damage it did to our homes but something else appeared to be going on. I just couldn't tell what. The uneasy feeling I had before the storm returned. My stomach felt like it did when I rode in the back seat of our car, queasy, not throwing up but close to it.

I loved my school mostly because of all of my friends and kind, patient teachers. They had funny names like my grandmotherly fifty-year-old first- and second-grade teacher, Mrs. Brockley; it sounded like the vegetable but without the second "o." With her rosy cheeks, plumpness and warm smile I felt quite sure she was Mrs. Santa Claus in disguise. And how would we ever know for sure because of the two-week break over the Christmas holiday? She could have easily had a second job. There was the fourth-grade teacher, stocky and bald Mr. Goodrick (not the company named Goodrich that Dad bought tires from) who, I heard from the older kids taught the best art classes ever. One student proudly showed off his creation that was about the size of a big Tootsie Roll—a sawdusty-clay thing that looked much like something our dog deposited in the backyard. I seriously questioned his artistic abilities.

But mostly I really liked our principal of Sunrise Elementary School, Mr. Shine. To a young girl, he looked as tall as a tree, yet moved swiftly like a deer and had eyes in the back of his head, just like my mom. He always had a grin on his face like he actually enjoyed being with us. Except his grin disappeared on the morning in second grade when he expelled me.

The immediate expulsion travesty resulted from a shoving and hitting episode with my best friend since first grade, but now my ex-best friend, Karen. She obviously resented the temporary responsibility and authority given to me by the custodian during morning recess. He asked and trusted me to stand guard over huge, easy-to-roll metal pipes stored in our play shed for the short term. I felt proud knowing my temporary guardianship would prevent obvious harm to a classmate if attempting to play on or around the dangerous pipes.

Karen wanted to play on the pipes pretending she was a log roller at the annual Timber Linn Fourth of July competitions. There was no sign of second-grade teacher, Mrs. Brockley to run inference, but under no uncertain terms was Karen going to get on those pipes on my watch. I explained my temporary role and when I firmly said, "Don't you dare get on those pipes," that led to her flash of defiance in her dark brown eyes, her first shove and the entire sordid episode escalated. The untimely entrance of the other third-grade teacher, seemingly more ancient than Mrs. Brockley, at least sixty-years old, plus slightly hunchbacked, Mrs. Safely, who saw only my retaliation in the hitting match, grabbed me by my upper right arm and Karen by her left as she marched us down to Mr. Shine's office. Before my parents arrived to hear the sordid details of the actions of their first child, their only darling daughter—which I hoped they would remember—I talked fast and explained that my dad always told me I could hit somebody back if they hit me first. "She started it," and "It's not my fault," didn't help. Mrs. Safely didn't care about my excuses or pleas for leniency. She certainly didn't know me well nor that I was the oldest and only girl in my family, therefore always in charge and bossing around my younger brothers and neighborhood children.

Apparently, my dad's personal survival philosophy didn't matter to the principal either. Mrs. Brockley stood, shaking her head seemingly mortified that two of her favorite students were duking it out in the play shed. And to make it even worse, we were girls, certainly not the typical behavior for ladies, even very young ones. Evidently it was expected for boys. Back in our classroom, while I was picking up my coat and Roy Rogers lunchbox before heading home since we'd been expelled for the remainder of the day, she pulled off and purposely dropped both of our paper red apples with our names printed boldly in black, from her "apple tree of goodness." I felt a twinge of remorse about the fiasco but knew I was in the right. I felt worse about having my apple on the floor, which was a first for me. It didn't even have a wormhole like most ones for the bad boys in the class. It was Mrs. Brockley's not-so-subtle psychological control over us for behavioral issues. I forgave Mr. Shine as he welcomed me back the following morning with his familiar grin and a hug.

In my third-grade class there were twenty-three pupils. That's what my teacher called us—pupils.

Most of us had spent the first and second grades together, like my ex-best friend Karen, who lived down the street, across the railroad tracks and around the corner in a gray and blue house with big windows, which now I avoided when walking to school. This new year I would sit right behind Lenny Oswald because my last name started with an R. We had a Kennedy, Johnson and Oswald in our class. The next year on November 21, 1963, the odd happenstance of these classmates' last names seemed eerie when President Kennedy had been shot by Lee Harvey Oswald and Vice President Lyndon Johnson became president.

On the second day back to school after the storm the bell blared. Miss Jonas, my third-grade teacher, who was tall, skinny, with wrinkled arms and hands plus a sharp pointed nose, said firmly but in a hushed tone, "Hurry students and be quiet. This is just a drill but it might not be one day." My classmates and I followed the square yellow emergency signs on the wall, quickly scurrying down the tiled ramp into the underground tunnel of my elementary school. We were headed to the bomb shelter.

Something scary was going on between our country, a little country off the southeast coast of ours called Cuba, and a big country across the world called Russia. We heard that huge missiles were pointed at us. Bad guys were always dressed in black. That's how they looked on our black and white television and the pictures they showed of Russian and Cuban people.

When we returned to our desks and got settled down, Miss Jonas said something that I have always remembered, "You are probably a little frightened like I am. But think about the pupils just like you in Cuba." I did think about the children living there: Did they attend school like me? Did they know that their country was taking on the United States? What would happen to them if these rockets were launched? I wondered what they really knew. My teacher said they didn't have television like we did. I thought about them for years.

Decades Later

Driving one hundred miles south on Highway 1 from Miami to Key West in our sporty rental car with longtime friend Carol, our first stop for seafood and Key Lime pie would be at the Couch Republic Sea-food Company. Carol had attended a conference in Miami and invited me to join her plus the road trip to the Keys, a place she'd always wanted to visit. One of my made-up beatitudes is, "Blessed are the curious for they shall have escapades." New exploits always worked for me.

After scrumptious fresh shrimp prepared four different ways—Cajun, beer-battered, garlic butter and coconut, we walked a few blocks to where millions have stood at the southernmost point in the continental United States at the concrete red, black and yellow marker on the corner of South and Whitehead Streets that reads "90 Miles to Cuba." I realized that I stood closer to Cuba than Miami, one hundred miles to the north. I had a flashback to my childhood school days walking down the hallway to the bomb shelter. I thought about those children who were probably as scared as I was during the Cuban

186

Missile Crisis that President Kennedy averted. I pondered how many people my age still living in Cuba recalled that time. I shared with Carol my recollection and she told me what she remembered. She had been attending high school in eastern Washington State and they had emergency drills, too.

Living on the west coast, all I basically knew about Cuban people was what I heard on the news. I questioned why thousands would risk their lives trying to escape through shark-infested waters in inner tube contraptions, homemade boats and little rafts of old tires roped together. I'd seen many photos in the news and each attempt showed desperation, ingeniousness and determination. One broadcast showed a 1950s blue convertible roped to inner tubes crammed with Cubans floating to Miami, hoping the currents would take them in the right direction. Another newscast showed an old green Chevy truck converted probably from a street cruiser to a water cruiser bobbing in the waves. It reminded me of my husband's first truck that, while he was in high school, he and his dad restored. Many were stopped by the U.S. Coast Guard and returned to Cuba. I'd read many people were in prison for speaking against the government and they had a dictator as president. But I wanted to know why they would jeopardize their lives, and those of their loved ones, to escape this small Caribbean country and flee to their closest neighbor, the United States. Could it really be that bad? I needed to know, so I started reading.

One article I read pointed out that when Fidel Castro seized power in 1959, this started a steady stream of Cuban refugees attempting to escape the communist regime. For our part, the U.S. welcomed each successful attempt with mostly open arms until then-President Clinton amended the 1966 Cuban Adjustment Act in 1994. It was called Wet Foot, Dry Foot which gave Cuban arrivals in the U.S. residency even if they didn't have visas. Since then, only Cuban refugees who made it to land had been granted political asylum until President Obama changed it in early 2017. The White House announced "Effective immediately, Cuban nationals who attempt to enter the United States illegally and do not qualify for humanitarian relief will be subject to removal, consistent with U.S. law and enforcement priorities. By taking this step, we are treating Cuban migrants the same way we treat migrants from other countries." Cuba had tied themselves to the Soviet Union and with its fall in 1991, economic conditions in Cuba suffered dramatically and thousands of Cubans took flight again in anything that floated.

I recalled the pathetic ordeal over a five-year-old boy named Elián González. In November 1999, he and his mother escaped in an overloaded flimsy inner tube raft with eleven others. It sank, drowning her and most other adults. He and two others were found about sixty miles north of Miami clinging to the inner tube where the U.S. Coast Guard spotted them. He ended up in Florida with relatives who fought to keep him in the U.S., his mother's dying wish.

His father, Juan Miguel, and other relatives lived in Cuba. This started a tug-of-war between Elián's U.S. relatives and his father which resulted with then-president, Fidel Castro, siding with the father. The Miami-based Cuban exile community backed family members in Florida. Media camped outside the home where Elián lived, with cameras constantly on him and his relatives. The case sparked a debate about parental rights. President Clinton's administration ultimately backed the father's rights and allowed him to take his son back to Cuba. His Miami family wouldn't give him up but on April 22, 2000 we watched on television when agents rushed with guns drawn to find a terrified little boy hunkered down in a closet. Hauled out at gunpoint by U.S. federal agents, it was a sad spectacle with, to me, a poor little boy used as a political pawn.

Fifteen years later to the day, I watched an interview with Elián on the news. At twenty-one years-old, he boasted being a member of Cuba's Militant Union of Young Communists and studying industrial engineering at the University of Matanzas near his home in Cárdenas, about ninety minutes outside Havana. The media reported that he practices karate, swims, goes to the movies and hangs out with friends. Elián spoke out about the U.S. embargo, and speaking to reporters at a youth congress in Ecuador in 2013, he said the economic blockade imposed by the American government caused his mother to risk her life and his so desperately in 1999. "Cuba, even with all its problems, has progressed over the years," he said. When asked where he would like to go if he could travel anywhere in the world, he replied without hesitation, "Los Estados Unidos," the United States. "I want the time to give my love to American people," he added in broken English. He recalled the trauma when the boat capsized, "I remember when I was put on the raft and my mom was covering me and I was raising my head, looking around…and at some point I raised my head and I didn't see her again. I was alone in the middle of the sea." I shed a tear for this young man.

When Cuban news occurred, my ears perked up and I paid attention. In 2015, Elián had been spotted at President Raúl Castro's closing speech to the Council of States, only three days after the historic announcement to restore diplomatic ties between the U.S. and Cuba. This intrigued me and I hoped it was a step in the right direction.

I agreed with then-President Obama when, on December 17, 2014, he said that Cold War-era policy of the past had failed and now seemed the right time to chart a new course in Cuba. America's forty-eight-year economic embargo had failed to bring change to that island and he hoped Cuba would move towards embracing democratic values, including freedom of speech and religion, on the path towards launching better relations with the United States. "The policy we've had in place for fifty years hasn't worked the way we wanted it to—the Cuban people are not free," President Obama said. But after the actions taken by his administration, including lifting travel restrictions for Cuban-Americans, Obama said he would be looking for reciprocal moves by the Cuban government before taking additional steps.

In 2016, more progress had been made including the first direct mail flights between the U.S. and Cuba for the first time in fifty years. I listened to the president's speech on March 20, 2016 when he and his family visited Cuba. I agreed with this decision and felt an odd sense of relief that finally an

American president was visiting Cuba, the first president in nearly ninety years.

Three months later I would learn first-hand the answers I had sought for years.

Cuba, Who Would Have Thought?

My ninety-year-old mother didn't want me to go. I reminded her it was her fault. She had instilled "Wanderlust" in me, a strong desire for, or impulse to wander or travel and explore the world. My ninety-one-year-old father said he wished he could go with me. My husband thought I shouldn't pass up the chance even though he wasn't interested in going. A few friends asked if I felt nervous about going to communist Cuba. Definitely NO! And I'd already been to Russia which had been a thoroughly en-lightening and educational adventure. This Cuba opportunity I would not pass up.

I loved the quote, "The world is a book, and those who do not travel read only a page." Time for an additional page exploring an old country yet new for me and on a new cruise line. Plus, I felt obligated to go, doing this for my occupation as a part-time travel agent—to learn more about Fathom Cruise Line and Cuba. I fully intended to take home what I learned to share with others about the people and, to most Americans, this somewhat mystifying island neighbor.

Why in the world did I choose to fly out on a red-eye to Newark, New Jersey to get to Miami? Instead of diagonal, I headed straight across the country then down, the long way. It was the only flight to Miami from PDX (Portland, Oregon) that would get me to the airport by eleven o'clock the next morning.

As we dropped from thirty-five thousand feet getting closer and closer to Newark, the sun popped up from the Atlantic Ocean. Out my window I could see we were flying over the New York harbor where, glistening in the morning sunbeams, stood the Statue of Liberty next to Ellis Island. I had visited Ms. Liberty two years earlier. Due to Hurricane Sandy's destruction, Ellis Island had been closed. A brief moment later we were parallel with the one hundred two-story, art deco Empire State Building that I've ascended twice, once on each visit to The City; there's only one "CITY" according to locals and they don't call it The Big Apple, thank you very much. I easily recognized the shiny silver, spired, Chrysler Building. The sky looked crowded with helicopters, big and small planes and below, the river seemed jam-packed with boats, barges and ferries. We were close enough that people appeared like busy ants bustling from one place to the next.

Each time I flew in I glanced in the direction on the Hudson River where a U.S. Airways flight had taken off from New York's LaGuardia airport on January 15, 2009. The plane made an emergency landing on the river after it struck a flock of Canada geese during its initial climb. The bird strike caused both engines to quickly lose power resulting in a controlled ditching where the plane ended up on the river. All one hundred and fifty passengers and crew miraculously survived thanks to expert pilots who safely glided the plane onto the water. The pictures of the plane floating on the river with people standing on the wings being rescued just in the nick of time by local watercraft as the partially submerged aircraft scarily sank into the river are still are seared into my memory banks. The incident became known as the "Miracle on the Hudson" and later, glued to the TV while listening to the black box recorder of the incident, I sat astounded how professional and calm the captain sounded. I spoke with our friend Russ, a seasoned pilot for Delta, who said the pilots handled it just as they should, and that all pilots are trained for these types of situations.

What a fabulous start to a new day. Who cared about only two hours of sleep off-and-on because of reading a twenty-five-cent book purchased at the annual library book sale? My bargain novel, *Castaway*, is the true story of a man and a woman who purposely stranded themselves on a deserted south sea island off the northernmost coast of Australia between May 1981 and June 1982. It reminded me of Jane Austin's style of writing, yet a combination of Robinson Crusoe and Swiss Family Robinson.

For this trip, I thought it prudent to carry on only one suitcase, thus adhering to my resolve to pack light. My connection was only thirty-five minutes and who knew where the next gate would be. I paid the extra $89 to upgrade to a seat closer to the exit and hopefully those around me would kindly let me off first. The next gate turned out to be thirty-seven gates away and in a different wing of the terminal.

I had my one personal item, a sizable Eagle Creek blue tote bag in which I stuffed my purse and important items I always carry in my personal bag for any crisis, emergency or just in case: sanitizing wipes, sleep aids, pen, pencil and notepad, gum, inflatable lumbar pillow, eye mask, earplugs, compression socks, and shawl or large scarf that works as a blanket to wrap up or throw over my head. And finally, my one carry-on suitcase, the largest that would legally fit, packed with cruise clothing but unlike clothing I'd taken on dozens of other cruises. This would be the most casual cruise I'd ever taken except to the Galapagos Islands five years earlier where we serendipitously met Jon and Beth, now dear friends. I've always hoped that on any trip I'd meet someone who'd impact my life somehow and maybe I would theirs. They have. With no formal dinner nights, I wouldn't need the black formal dresswear, glitzy shoes or blingy jewelry. Nope, I had cotton items like capris and breathable blouses. I had casual mix-and-match clothing that could be worn a few times and with the off-chance of spillage, I could use the complimentary laundry.

I didn't need soaps or shampoo as they were furnished. I didn't need a jacket or umbrella because the weather forecast showed ninety degrees with one thousand percent humidity (I am sometimes prone to exaggeration), really one hundred percent, but being from Oregon we are not accustomed to humidity. I had sturdy Keen walking sandals, along with another pair to switch out, basic underclothing, sleepwear, passport, travel confirmation, guidebook, laminated tri-fold map of Cuba, language guide, copies of travel documents, credit card (even though I wouldn't be able to use it in Cuba), plenty of cash in Euros as our U.S. Dollar imposed an exchange fee, emergency contact info, medical insurance card, list of meds, travel insurance, three postcards showing my city and state, journal, extra pens and pencils (should have still taken more to give away), and my sense of humor.

I had my well-travelled purse, my beach-colored Baggalini bag that's lightweight and the cross-body design that keeps my hands clutter-free, mostly for shopping purposes. Plus, the founder of this label hailed from Oregon and started her own company in the mid 1990s—a true American success story. I had my phone charger, camera, extra battery and charger, extra memory card as one thousand might not be enough, small flashlight, binoculars for bird watching, alarm clock, headphones and Kindle for night-time reading to be courteous to my cruise-mate, who I would meet by midday on board.

On the next three-hour uneventful flight, I boned up on Cuban history that I gleaned from my two travel books. In 1492, a familiar date, Christopher Columbus sailed the ocean blue and encountered about one hundred thousand indigenous people in Cuba. On arrival, he saw dwellings and wrote, "Looking like tents in a camp. All were of palm branches, beautiful constructed." The Taínos Indians were skilled weavers, potters, boat builders and fisherman. Columbus wrote, "They are the best people in the world, without knowledge of evil nor do they murder or steal, that these people show is the most singularly loving behavior, gentle and always laughing."

However, the Spaniards changed this. They were on a quest for silver and gold and when the Spanish

Crown financed ships there had to be a return. Taínos were sent to work in mines and on plantations. Slavery became explicitly forbidden by the Catholic Church but by the end of the 16th century the entire indigenous population had died due to violence, being worked to death, and European diseases like measles, small pox and tuberculosis. This created the demand for slaves from Africa. Gosh, this history sounded familiar to what happened with our American Indians. Cuba became the most important stopover for Spanish ships and traders carrying the riches from the Americas back to Europe.

With its open harbors, Cuba became defenseless to criminals. Piracy Island became known as Haiti and the French colony located right next door had plenty of pirates, sugar and slavery. To defend itself, two castles (fortresses) were built and both were called Morro castle: one in Havana and the other in Santiago de Cuba. On July 1, England attacked Morro Castle in Santiago de Cuba and by July 29, the British flag of St. George flew over the city. Cuba was now under English control and the first thing they accomplished was to lift Spain's trade restrictions creating more economic opportunities for everyone. The occupation only lasted eleven months because sugar planters from Jamaica pressured England to give Cuba back to Spain—they didn't want any other rivals in the English sugar industry. In February 1763 the English swapped Cuba back to Spain for Florida in the Treaty of Paris. By this time Spain had a more enlightened king, Charles III, who kept the free trade policy and ten years later, after the swap, the U.S. started trading directly with Cuba. Spain had sunk much money into Havana,

196

specifically the architecture in the parks, courtyards, libraries and paved streets. The pictures in my travel books showed buildings that looked similar to ones we saw some years earlier in Cartagena, Colombia and all over Spain.

Slavery began in 1513 and it didn't stop until 1890. Slaves from west African tribes formed forty-five percent of Cuba's population. They arrived the same way as slaves did to America: a brutal journey across the Atlantic, chained up, overcrowded, and many dying from starvation and disease. But Cuba's story seemed different and unlike ours in North America—ethnic groups were kept together, the result of traditions like music and religious beliefs being retained, passed down and kept intact. Santería, the worship of the saints, became deeply entrenched over three hundred years and more widespread than Catholicism. Another difference between Cuba and North America was that slaves could buy their own and their family's freedom, and could buy property.

Cuba needed slaves because sugar became a huge money-making industry. Ten years after England lifted Spain's trade restrictions, Cuba and the U.S. were trading, and because of this the North American sweet tooth boomed and it expanded ten-fold. Even before the sugar surge, the U.S. had its eye on Cuba. After the Louisiana purchase, Cuba's location at the mouth of the Mississippi and Gulf of Mexico had strategic importance. In 1808, Thomas Jefferson attempted to purchase Cuba from Spain, then James Polk offered one hundred million, Franklin Pierce offered one hundred thirty million and his successor,

James Buchanan, tried to purchase Cuba twice for the same price. Spain said no each time.

Spain hung on to Cuba, but barely. Semana Bolivariana led wars of independence in other South American countries and by 1835 the Spanish only had Cuba left. Young Cuban patriots were making their voices heard. Spain responded by exiling or executing these leading nationalists. Tensions were high and after the American Civil War, Spain continued losing its grip on Cuba because slavery had been abolished in the U.S. on December 18, 1865.

In 1868 a planter, Carlos Manuel de Céspedes, freed all the slaves on his plantation and gave them the opportunity of freedom or to fight with him against the Spanish. Other planters did the same thing and within one week fifteen hundred men flocked to his call, assembled, and were ready to fight. The Ten Years War started. Cuba found itself caught in their first war for independence and white and black peasant farmers fought side-by-side against one hundred thousand Spanish soldiers. The freedom fighters in this war were called the Mambís and some of their leaders were Salvador Cisneros, Máximo Gómez and Antonio Maceo. They liberated much of the island; however, ten years later, the movement collapsed and the forces signed a peace treaty. In another ten years, the entire Cuban economy was devastated with huge tracks of land abandoned. North American investors bought up these ravished sugar plantations at extremely low rates. Under Spanish domination things returned to what had been normal. However, independence became the cause that united all Cubans. An intellectual and protestor named José Martí had been exiled to Spain after being in prison on the Isle of Pines where Fidel Castro spent time in the same prison. He had not been discouraged in the previous struggles for independence. José, after having spent several very productive years abroad, settled in the U.S. and formed the Cuban Revolutionary Party in 1892. He effectively campaigned to promote social change in Cuba. Little by little Martí won over key figures, like generals. He offered solutions for the conflicts that had arisen between the civilian and military authorities in the past wars. In 1895 he joined General Maximo Gómez in the Dominican Republic and together they sailed to Cuba. They met up with José Maceo and together they instigated the War of Independence. One month later Martí died in combat on May 19, 1895. His motto declared, "To die for the fatherland is to live."

Once the U.S. entered the war it became the Spanish-Cuban-American War. I'd always heard it referred to as the Spanish-American war and didn't even realize it had taken place on Cuban soil—so much for retaining American history. Teddy Roosevelt lead a cavalry charge on San Juan Hill in Santiago de Cuba and the role of Mambíses was downplayed. On July 3, the U.S. Navy decimated the Spanish as it attempted to escape Santiago harbor, the exact same harbor we'd be sailing in and out of in several days. On July 17, Spain surrendered, their flag lowered and the United States stars and stripes were raised. This enabled the U.S. to take possession of Cuba, Puerto Rico and the Philippines with very little effort. After the war, the U.S. occupied Cuba for three years until May 20, 1902, granting Cuba its independence. Over the next fifty years the U.S. basically supported crooked presidents based on financial interests and the whims of Congress, corporations and lobbyists. Cuban women began to organize and achieve the vote, founding the Women's Club of Cuba in 1918. U.S. interests in sugar went from fifteen to seventy-five percent. As a result of prohibition, people flocked to Havana. Eighty percent of all buildings in Havana were constructed from the end of the Spanish-Cuban-American war to 1959. A lot appeared to be going on in the infrastructure of Cuba and although presidents were corrupt, much money was being funneled into social services. These crooked presidents turned into extremely rich men and fled their country.

Enter Fulgencio Batista who ran for election and won. At first he gave the impression of being benevolent: He started social reforms and had a free-thinking attitude towards the public and the welfare of workers' rights. During his term, Cuba entered World War II as a minor ally of the U.S. and sold all its sugar to the U.S. which rose from almost three million tons in 1939 to over four million in 1944. This increase led to a prolonged sugar cane harvest, which along with other factors, led to a decline in the number of workers' strikes under Batista. But he also retired to Florida a wealthy man. After Batista, poor leadership ushered in a decade of disorder and gangster violence with mob-run hotels. In 1952, Batista returned and ran for election again. Likely to lose, he led a coup d'état and seized power three months before the election.

Fidel Castro, a practically unknown twenty-five-year-old lawyer, initiated the popular insurrection against the dictatorship. He organized a large group of young people, nearly all of whom were unemployed or workers of humble origins. They trained in secret and on July 6, 1953, then attacked two army garrisons. More than fifty of the young rebels were captured or surrendered and were savagely murdered by the army. Public opinion and the rapid mobilization of the press saved the lives of the other young revolutionaries. Fidel Castro had been sentenced to fifteen years in prison and brother Raúl sentenced to thirteen, other rebels receiving less. Batista won an electoral farce in 1954 and was forced to grant amnesty to Fidel and his compañeros. Then there were more struggles and fighting. The climax of the revolutionary war came when Che Guevara's column liberated the city of Santa Clara, capital of the central province. After derailing an armored train that Batista had hurriedly sent from Havana to halt the rebels' advance and while Fidel and Raúl's forces besieged the cities of Santiago de Cuba and Guantanamo, Batista fled the country on January 1, 1959.

In cahoots with the U.S. embassy, Batista's military high command had drawn up contingency plans for preventing the triumph of the revolutionary forces but they were useless when Fidel called a general strike that brought the country to a standstill. In the early days of the revolution military structures were dismantled, war criminals were put on trial and measures benefiting Cubans were adopted. Among other changes, telephone rates were reduced, rents on houses and apartments were cut by fifty percent, the consumption of Cuban-made products increased and homes were built for people with low incomes. Private beaches were opened to the public, considerable resources were allocated for public health and education and many of the old army garrisons were turned into schools. Large cattle ranches were nationalized and next were the sugar plantations. United Fruit Company, major newspapers and the opposition television stations were next to be nationalized.

The Agrarian Reform Law highlighted the class disparities within Cuban society and quickened growing conflicts with the United States government. In 1959, the CIA considered a comprehensive plan of subversion against the Cuban government. The U.S. sponsored training camps in central America for Cuban exiles, preparing them to invade the island. A few months later, the Catholic hierarchy in Cuba began an anticommunist campaign. The U.S. set about destabilizing the government including threats to cut off Cuba's fuel supply. Because foreign-owned refineries refused to process the oil Cuba acquired from the Soviet Union, the revolutionary government nationalized those companies on June 28, 1960. In response, the U.S. eliminated Cuba's sugar quota, hoping to crush the country by closing off its main market. Basically as retaliation, Cuba proceeded to nationalize all American interests on the island, including banks, factories, mines, telephone and electricity companies and the railroad. All Cuban and foreign-owned companies with more than twenty-five workers were also nationalized. On October 19, the U.S. banned all trade with Cuba.

Relations between our two countries deteriorated even further. Officials at the State Department and the CIA attempted to push Castro from power. In April 1961, the CIA launched what its leaders believed would be the definitive strike: a full-scale invasion of Cuba by fourteen hundred American trained Cubans who had fled their homes when Castro took over. From what I gathered from the history book, the plans were somehow known by Castro, and a frustrated President Kennedy began to suspect that the plan the CIA had promised would be "both clandestine and successful" might in fact be "too large to be clandestine and too small to be successful." But it was too late to stop and on April 17, the U.S.-backed Cuban exile brigade began its invasion at an isolated spot on the island's southern shore known as the Bay of Pigs. Almost immediately, the invasion was a disaster. The CIA tried to keep it a secret but a radio station on the beach, which the agency's reconnaissance team had failed to spot, broadcast every detail of the operation to listeners across Cuba. Backup paratroopers landed in the wrong place. Before long, Castro's troops had pinned the invaders on the beach and the exiles surrendered after less than a day of fighting with one hundred fourteen killed and over eleven hundred taken prisoner. The CIA and Cuban exile brigade believed that President Kennedy would eventually allow the American military to intervene in Cuba on their behalf. However, Kennedy stood firm—as much as he did not want to "abandon Cuba to the communists," he said he would not start a fight that might end in World War III.

In November 1961, President Kennedy approved an operation that would provide a ruse for direct U.S. military involvement. But Kennedy never went so far as to provoke an outright war. Operation Mongoose stopped short by an emergency which took the world to the verge of an atomic conflict that I recalled as a child: The Cuban Missile Crisis. This crisis became the most dangerous in the entire history of the Cold War between the U.S. and the Soviet Union. On October 22, 1962 when the U.S. intelligence services discovered that medium-range Soviet ballistic missiles had been installed in Cuba, President Kennedy demanded their immediate withdrawal. He also instituted a naval blockade of Cuba. The missiles had been put in under a secret agreement between Havana and Russia. They signed it in August 1962 to discourage direct U.S. military intervention in Cuba.

After a week of threats from President Kennedy, the Soviet Union decided to remove their missiles. The Cuban government, unhappy about the fact that those negotiations were carried out behind its back, refused to allow its country to be inspected. The Cuban Missile Crisis ended with the U.S. giving a verbal assurance that it would not attack Cuba militarily. The Cuban Missile Crisis didn't help the already damaged American-Cuban-Soviet dealings. While these intense conflicts were taking place, in Cuba a massive literacy campaign started. It had spectacular results—in just a few months over seven hundred thousand people were taught how to read and write, dropping the illiteracy to less than four percent, the lowest illiteracy rate in Latin America. Private education stopped on June 6, 1961, and all private schools were nationalized. With the agreement of all Latin American governments, except Mexico, the U.S. expelled Cuba from the Organization of American States in January 1962, which led to Cuba's diplomatic isolation. On February 7, 1962, the U.S. placed an embargo to include all imports.

I needed to retain some of this history as we would be visiting many famous locations, seeing many monuments and statues of these famous and important Cuban heroes. Plus, it explained how we got involved in The Cuban Missile Crisis. That's what I cared about. I vowed to read more about this time in history when I returned home.

The Newark to Miami flight went by quickly and I felt pretty certain of the education I'd received from my American books. But I really wanted to speak with Cuban people and learn what they knew. I also decided to look for a book about Cuba's history and read it from their eyes. I've learned over the years that "there are two sides to every story." Or more.

The flight landed on time and walking out of the terminal I was hit with hot sticky air. After hailing a taxi, we were on our way to a newly installed cruise terminal where the taxi driver had never been. He said, "It's a good day when you can learn something new." I totally agreed with him and asked him how long the ride would be. He said, "No road is long with good company." Translated means it took about twenty minutes and turned out to be one of the best taxi rides of my life.

Soft-spoken yet talkative, he used disjointed English, sometimes pausing to think of the words he wanted to verbalize. I complimented him on his efforts and told him I could easily understand him—not totally true—I just had to pay attention and listen more carefully.

I asked, "Where are you from originally?"

"Turkey, in the northern part."

"Do you have family in America?"

"A cousin. We joined him and his family three years ago. We live in my cousin's home. I hope to return to my homeland one day. There are too many political issues. I feared for the safety of my wife and baby son so we moved to America."

Some taxis have a window blocking the passenger from the driver. With none in this car, and sitting diagonally, I looked at the right side of his head of thick black hair. He glanced back quickly a couple of times while talking, not totally taking his eyes off the road. I liked him.

I told him we'd been in his country for only one day while on a Mediterranean cruise, nine years earlier. We'd toured historic, biblical Ephesus and surrounding areas. He shared that he and his wife had traveled from their home in Bursa, a city towards Istanbul, by train to Ephesus in 2001, to see Elton John perform at The Theatre, the exact same theater where THE Saint Paul had spoken to the Ephesians thousands of years before. He said they sat on the two thousand-year-old stones for three hours and would never forget "such a happening." I told him we sat in the same theater, minus the professional entertainment. Instead we had roving actors dressed in Roman attire carrying swords and shields.

It had been their first time visiting so they toured the same ancient ruins like we did. We shared the awe-inspiring feeling walking up the stone steps and seeing the enormous Celcus Library, made of white marble. I recalled looking down and seeing imprints of feet pressed into the stone from countless people who walked these same steps over thousands of years. He said he'd taken off his shoes and walked in the actual steps. He reminisced about seeing the Bath of Varius, built of blocks of marble and the mosaics in the forty-meters long corridor; the Temple of Isis, just broken blocks with no pillars remaining; the Hercules Gate, called that because one can still see the relief of Hercules on it.

I felt temporarily transported to Ephesus from his vivid recollections. He generated a craving to return to spend more time wandering this significant, ancient city. We agreed that these people were ingenious to create such an infrastructure with few tools and no equipment other than strong human and animal backs. We shared separate memories, special to each of us but even more as we'd revealed them to each other. While unloading my one piece of luggage, he shook his head and commented that one suitcase for a woman was a new experience for him. I chuckled and decided not to try to enlighten him on my philosophy of packing light. I paid, generously tipped and thanked my nameless Turkish acquaintance and wished him a good life.

At the port check-in, I sat next to a woman and struck up a conversation. She originally hailed from New York State but had lived in the Miami area for many years. Fran had a strong eastern accent; I wouldn't forget her name because my middle name is Frances. We were greeted by Adonia staff and soon hundreds of us were onboard Fathom Cruise Line's first and only ship. After finding my stateroom complete with a nice big square window, I wandered around the ship to get familiar with the layout, as I did before any cruise. Turned out, Fran's room was right next to mine. I received a text from my soon-to-be-roommate, Carole Lee; she made it onboard. We met up, acting like long-lost cousins. Time for some sustenance, we headed to the Welcome Buffet for seafood and salads and got acquainted. As we cruised out of the calm waters of Miami's harbor, passing high-rise condos and apartments with boats of every kind in the azure water that Sunday afternoon, I recalled my favorite cruise slogan by Roselle Mercier Montgomery, "Never a ship sails out of the bay but carries my heart as a stowaway."

That afternoon, roommate Carole Lee and I talked about our expectations of this voyage. As travel professionals representing our separate agencies, we were paired up for the week. We'd become quick friends via Facebook and knew we'd be compatible. She told me that some of her Cuban-American friends weren't happy she'd come on this trip and explained why: They had their own traumatic stories about their escapes, creating a new life had been extremely difficult, and concerns for those family and friends left behind in Cuba due to many factors. It had been a challenging decision for her to visit this country but she felt it important to make her own judgments. It seemed like many on this trip were doing the same thing—coming to their own conclusions and maybe, hopefully, making a small difference for the future. I hoped this wasn't naïve on my part. I told her one of my favorite things is to go where I've never been and I told her about my childhood school memories. Lao Tzu said, "A journey of a thousand miles must begin with a single step." I had taken that single step and would be in Cuba the next morning.

Not Just Another Caribbean Island

Squinting at my travel alarm, it read seven o'clock. I jumped out of bed afraid I would miss something but quietly so not to rouse my roomie. While getting dressed in lightweight cotton capris and a floral blouse on Monday morning, knowing we were getting closer to the Caribbean island country, I thought of my friend Noel, who volunteered like me once a week at Meals on Wheels as a server and greeter. He told me at age nineteen he had been stationed at Homestead Air Force Base for three months during The Cuban Missile Crisis. They scheduled flights of planes loaded with weapons over Cuba every day just in case they were needed.

Forgetting breakfast, I went quickly up to deck ten where squawking sea gulls were circling our ship. With their red bills and black heads with a strip of black down their backs and tails, they looked different and much more interesting than ones in Oregon. When the Adonia cruised into the entrance of the narrow Havana harbor June 12, 2016, my childhood memories of the third-grade practice drills hiding in school tunnels came flooding back. At eight o'clock, standing on ship's deck and already dripping with perspiration, I asked myself why I'd chosen to come to the Caribbean in the summer: Curiosity—originating in the third grade, I reminded myself.

Our medium-size ship slowly sailed through a constricted entrance to Havana with two fortresses perched across from each other on the hillsides. Farther down toward the city, on the right, I spotted a gigantic white man that appeared to be hundreds of feet tall. As I unsnapped the small camera case, the lens on my Sony fogged up. While waiting for it to un-steam, I pulled out my Cuba travel guide for information to use when there is no live, speaking guide nearby. I always obtained travel guides and books before each trip, often gifts from my husband, as he knew I liked to be prepared and know as much as possible about the history, people, foods and shopping before I arrived. My philosophy has always been if you are spending thousands of dollars on an adventure of a lifetime, spend $15 to $20 and get a good book or two so you'll know what you're getting yourself into.

As we got closer, I recognized the immense, white, glowing man as Jesus, welcoming me and others to this country. He looked fairly new standing on top of a hill. My *DK Eyewitness Travel Guide: Cuba* paperback book reported, "The statue was carved from white Carrara marble. He is 66-feet high including a 10-foot base and weighs about 320 tons. He was built from 67 blocks of marble that had been brought from Italy after being personally blessed by Pope Pius XII. Christ is standing with his right hand near his chin and left hand near his chest. Facing the city, the statue was left with empty eyes to give the impression of looking at all, from anywhere to be seen. It was inaugurated on La Cabana Hill in the suburb of Casablanca on Christmas Eve 1958. Fifteen days after its dedication, on January 8, 1959, Fidel Castro entered Havana during the Cuban Revolution." Shocked to see Jesus, I thought that a communist country meant certainly everyone must be an atheist. This became the first of many incorrect, preconceived notions.

Seeing the red, white and blue flag flying on a Cuban navy ship, the colors were the same as our American flag but with five blue and white stripes and one white star in the middle of a red triangle. Dozens of tall multicolored buildings, domes and spires towered over the hundreds of shorter dwellings and statues.

Excitement grew for me as people, dozens of all ages, were waving from the banks and docks, and standing on the rooftops of their homes and garages. I waved back and tried to contain myself from jumping up and down. Every other car on the road appeared to be from the 1950s and early '60s. Not only vehicles but horse-drawn carriages, onion-domed gold Russian orthodox churches, Catholic churches and unhurried people, were all visible from the vantage point on the tenth floor of Adonia. Fathom Cruise Lines had been granted approval to take people-to-people educational tours to Cuba and was the first American cruise line to take visitors; only its third trip to Cuba and it included me. A pilot boat guided us in to San Francisco pier conveniently right across the street from the square with the same name. I couldn't wait to get off the ship and start

211

exploring and meeting people, maybe someone who remembered The Cuban Missile Crisis.

I'd done my homework just like I had on all vacations before. Cuba is seven hundred fifty miles long and fifty-five miles wide and the largest island in the Caribbean. It's a bit smaller than Pennsylvania, and my state of Oregon is twice as big as Pennsylvania. There are over eleven million people and it is a socialist country but the political party is communism. It is known for white-sand beaches, rolling mountains, cars, cigars and rum.

Havana - Day Uno

Immediately we were socked with ninety degrees and one hundred percent humidity but I didn't care; I knew I'd be sweaty. I doubted the round purple #17 sticker affixed to my blouse indicating my tour group would stay on. I passed through the white-walled immigration station with other passengers and received a new stamp in my passport and exchanged Euros for Cucs (Cuban Convertible Peso). It was an easy exchange and about one Euro equaled one Cuc. We were told that sensors were built in the wall to take one's temperature but it was never explained why. I sauntered in and wondered, if I'd had a fever, would they have detained me.

Ernesto was our guide for the afternoon. He stood about five feet eight inches tall, had coal black hair, tanned complexion and medium build. He had a self-confident, pleasant bright white smile that infected me with internal warmth. He would spend time with us in Old Havana on a slow-paced walking tour. When he welcomed us I instantly picked up on the pronunciation and heard him say "Cooba" not like I had learned, Cuba. I said it correctly from then on. Havana was pronounced "Habana" and I would say it that way the rest of the trip. Old Habana is a recognized UNESCO world heritage site and provides a glimpse into the history of this city built in the early 1500s.

Ernesto shepherded us directly across from the cruise dock down a narrow avenue and walking by colonial buildings with wrought iron terraces over-looking the cobblestone street reminded me of places we'd seen in Spain. Laundry hanging from railings reminded me of Italy and decrepit buildings that needed much repair reminded me of Greece. Colorful artwork, instead of undecipherable nonsensical graf-fiti at home, lined the tight street where only one car could maneuver. The narrow avenue poured out into San Francisco square, named for the convent next to it. He told us that the square was built in 1628 with the objective of supplying water to the ships trading with the city. Its historical significance was similar to our Ellis Island where immigrants were logged and registered after their arrival. He said Old Habana has four main squares. Today much of the old city is in ruins from years of neglect and weather, reducing many of the buildings in the heart of Habana to rubble. In some cases, facades stand as an empty reminder of 16th and 17th century colonial architect-ture that once stood proud. However, many parts of the city are under renovation. Students attending trade schools are tasked with the job and are using many of the same techniques that built the city. While students repair Old Habana's crumbling buildings, government workers have the job of updating its plumbing and electrical systems, an up-grading project long overdue.

Standing in the middle of San Francisco de Assisi Square, Ernesto pointed out the domed Lonja del Comercio building, a former commodities market built in 1909. Renovated in 1996, it provides office space for foreign companies. Next to it is a pictures-que fountain built in 1836 called Fuente de los Leones (Lions Fountain), made with white Carrara marble. Ernesto chatted about the role of religion as I resituated myself in the shade of the old cathedral. I learned years earlier when traveling in the summer to always find shade to hide from the blazing sun. Built in 1608, the church over the years has been joined by the fountain of lions and a bronze life-size statue of José María López Lledín, known as a gentleman from Paris and a famous street person in the 1950s. The statue's beard has been polished by the thousands of hands touching it for luck.

Off to one side in the square there looked to me to be a very out-of-place, modern art sculpture of a stick-figure gold man in a sitting position like his body was resting on an invisible chair. Gesturing with his hands he seemed to be speaking to another gold stick-creature. Cleverly taking a photo of the cathedral through the gold-pieced creations, I saw a couple across the square coming out of the church. She appeared to glide effortlessly dressed in a white, shimmery, poufy wedding dress. I surmised that the statue next to the church was St. Francis himself but our guide said no. St. Francis originally stood on top of the bell tower but he tumbled down in a cyclone in 1846. The statue today is of an Indian boy with no further explanation provided by Ernesto. The wedding couple posed with the statue, I figured probably for good luck.

The newest square is Plaza de Cathedral, aptly named for the Cathedral de San Cristobal which overshadowed this plaza. It's the home of artists and entrepreneurs who have set up shop in corridors with little stalls where frilly lace items, the distinct musky smell of leather goods, freshly varnished wood sculptures and trinkets were being sold. I learned something quickly about my new friend Fran—she loved to shop, as often as possible. She told me up front with a twinkle in the most glacier blue, piercing eyes I'd ever seen, "I'm a shopaholic—I've been to therapy off and on over the years. It worked, somewhat. Don't worry about me; I never get lost." She didn't even seem to breathe during her run-on sentences. This was the beginning of me nervously saying, "Fran, we're going . . . now!" Of slight build, and long, flowing grayish blond hair, she was shorter and much smaller than me and walked very fast.

That afternoon while in mid-sentence of Ernesto describing a historic fountain, she darted off and disappeared down a cobblestone avenue. I looked down the street and didn't see her. I mumbled to myself, well, she's an adult, and decided not to squeal on her to our tour guide. I also thought he'd seen her quick take-off. Then a couple of blocks later, she came back walking right beside me like she'd never left. This was the beginning of such behavior. She would catch up, never losing the group but laden with several bags crammed full of special handmade treasures for her husband and gifts for friends and family at home. And she smartly brought her own big reusable bags from home. This woman could teach lessons in how to shop efficiently and quickly. And I thought I was good. Her husband would be picking her up at the cruise ship terminal at the end of the trip, so this gave her the freedom to buy as much as she could carry off the ship. I quit fretting about her that afternoon after the two evaporations and reappearances.

Plaza Viega had once been home to some of Habana's wealthiest residents. I marveled at the varied architecture that filled this square. Built in 1559, the Old Square has some of the most superb stained glass in Cuba. The Square is part of a collaborative restoration project between the Gaspar Melchor de Jobellanos workshop school and the city historical manager. The school offers students wood and metal shops, a masonry studio, and teaches classes in mural painting and plastering. There is also a workshop for students to learn stained glass techniques utilizing wooden frames instead of metal. Colegio Santo Angel, a colonial house, collapsed in 1993. Restored, it's now home to El Santo Angel restaurant, as well as apartments. Casa de las Hermanas Cardenás, built in 1602, had been a colonial style building but is now a major institute of visual arts. Draped on wires stretched across walkways are dozens of before-and-after photos giving testimony to the hard work restoring these historical buildings. The buildings and squares that have been finished are splendid and now gathering places filled with cafés, restaurants and shops. We stopped by Taller Experimental de Gráfica to learn more about how creative Cubans are at crafting art using age-old equipment and tools. One man sat cutting scraps of old paper and creating artsy collages of animals and scenery. Another worked with pen and ink drawings on heavy paper. One woman, hunched over canvas, painted colorful buses and cars, some in watercolors, some oils. President Obama and his family visited the same place in 2016 on their historic visit. There hung an eleven-by-sixteen-inch photo of him, the Pope and Raúl Castro—the trio all dressed as superheroes and each one draped in a Superman cape. The presidents proudly displayed their countries' flags on their chests with contrasting red and blue capes, while the Pope looked like he always does, robed in white.

Outside a miniature brick-colored, short-haired Dachshund pranced around fetching attention outfitted in green camouflage military garb that resembled a Halloween costume. I had to stop to pet him as he reminded me of our second family dog, Little Red Duke, our Doxie we nicknamed Dukie. My younger brother (by three years) and I received our first inside house doggie as a get-well enticement really trying to distract us from how badly our throats felt while recovering from having our tonsils out. I still remember the first time I saw Dukie poking his little black nose out of the jacket my father wore. We squealed with delight but not too much for fear of damaging our already hurting throats. Now that I think about it, my guess is my parents used this excuse to extend the days of peace and quiet for as long as possible.

Not far away was a cigar-smoking woman who would gladly read your fortune and sell you cigars.

Our guide warned us not to purchase cigars from street people as the tobacco would likely be tea leaves or something less recognizable. We saw street performers dressed as metal statues, Star Wars characters and historical lookalikes. As I glanced around, I saw many colorful doors and speculated who and what might be behind them.

Coconuts, melons and some unrecognizable fresh produce were being sold by street vendors on every corner, including fresh juices and fruit kabobs on a stick. The sweet fruity smells reminded me I was in the tropics. I never found gelato or ice cream. Nor did I find any typical glass display cases found all over Europe chock full of puffy, gooey rolls or doughnuts, chunky cookies or any layered cakes with frosting or whipped cream. Gawking and taking in the sights as our guide Ernesto steered us through alleys and avenues, he shared insights about his country and the history. We stopped at O'Reilly street, which I thought peculiar since my maiden name is Riley. I didn't realize the Irish had lived in Cuba but then I hadn't realized a lot about Cuba. He pointed out a building that had been the former Cámara de Representantes, formerly the House of Representatives. They were moved to a safer, larger structure. The renovated columned building with its stunning exterior houses an elegant ballroom and is now a museum and cultural center.

We ate lunch at a government-owned restaurant. The interior had been redone in rich dark woods and, with good-size windows, appeared bright and airy. Obviously, this building had recently gone through a total gut-job and had been renovated beautifully. We were all extremely appreciative that air conditioning came blasting from wall units not far from where were we sitting. Waiters were polite, welcoming and spoke some English. Appearing without even asking were steamy chunks of marinated beef, white rice topped with saucy black beans, slices of mango and a green bean salad pleasantly displayed on yellow and brown oval platters. The first bite of beef tasted salty and just a bit spicy yet a little sweet with whatever combination of spices were used. Two beverages were included. I selected Diet Coke, actually called Tukola Dietética by Ciego Montero, and bottled still water. Somehow a mojito also materialized.

The Door

It worked out that I had sat at a table that was served first. Consequently, I finished lunch before many others. Some elected to remain in the air-conditioned building while I chose to meander around outside but not far with my mother's voice cemented in my brain, "Don't wander around, stay with the group!" Before our walking tour began again, nearby I saw a man exiting a blue and white door with iron scrollwork across the top. And he left it partially ajar. To me, it was all the invitation I needed; clearly it was a sign, the only sign I needed to take a peek to see what might be behind the colorful door.

Lo and behold, there was a lush green courtyard filled with orchids climbing up a stone wall, a squatty tree with lengthy sagging white trumpets, magenta bougainvillea, something that looked like a cousin to our gladiolus, a scarlet tree that could be on fire, and

219

crimson and pink hibiscus planted so closely together they were one big bush of velvety hues. There were tables and chairs fashioned out of black scrolled iron and several well-dressed people, one with a laptop with papers spread out between them. I felt transported by the combined fragrances to a memory of a perfumeria I visited three times in Paris.

Off to one side, two women wore similarly styled white dresses except around the bottom and scooped neckline, one trimmed in orange and the other in yellow. One sported a bright yellow scarf tied creatively through her hair and the other, a yellow cloth flower tucked carefully in the black braided hair swirled on the top of her head. They were crafting something and chatting in Spanish which I didn't understand. Even though reading ahead of time about the Afro-Cuban history, in my naïveté I didn't realize that there were so many dark-skinned people living in Cuba. I thought they were like me, Caucasian, just more tan. Again, I was so wrong.

I gently interrupted them with "Hola." They both smiled and greeted me in English—must have been my accent. Or maybe because I wore my cross-over purse layered with the cross-over water holder. Or maybe it was the quarter-size purple round #17 glued to my chest, a dead giveaway to them and all others, indicating my tour group. Like me, they were perspiring, which I thought might indicate that I wasn't the only one overheated.

One stated matter-of-factly, "You are from ship," not a question but a statement. I replied, "Si, may I watch you?" One replied, "Please sit," as the other sat threading the top of flat sticks together with heavy string making a fan. She then picked up a little homemade-looking hammer and bound the seventeen wood slats together at the bottom with a nail. The other painted brightly colored butterflies, hummingbirds or flowers. Ms. Orange used a little torch about the size of the ones at home when someone is burning the top of Crème Brûlée to etch some details and burned a cursive *Cuba* on the top slat.

They were sisters and had lived in the Habana area all their lives. Ms. Orange pulled out a wallet and showed me photos of her children and young grandbabies. The other, Ms. Yellow, had been widowed years earlier and they lived together, the taller yellow-dressed sister pointing to a house way down the street that she said was the one painted pink. Surprised they weren't sitting outside showing off their handcrafts, I mentioned that they were unique so others should see them. They both giggled shyly and Ms. Orange said they liked being hidden from the tourists and that her daughter operated a stall on another street where she sold their handmade fans and other wood-carved items. She seemed the more outgoing of the two and offered that they had a younger brother who lived in Florida. He went to college in 1983 and they hadn't seen him since the night he left. She said he went to Eastern Europe to study medicine then immigrated to the United States where he became a dentist. I didn't ask any questions but listened as she said that to purchase a visa to visit him in America was too costly but hoped he would return to them one day.

My first purchase in Cuba was one of their carefully crafted fans painted hot pink with an orange rose in the middle and *Cuba* burnt into the edge. A bargain at five Cucs, I paid ten. I thanked them for their time and said adios. The shorter sister said, "Muchas Gracias for coming to my country. I am hopeful about our countries' futures together and please return one day." Even though the sisters appeared in their sixties my guess is they were probably in their early fifties—clearly life wasn't easy for them. As I left I asked their names. Ms. Orange became Elena and Ms. Yellow was Yolanda. But I didn't get their last names. This began my resolve of "paying up" instead of trying to get a bargain and dickering on prices like I normally did on Mexican and other Caribbean trips. If items were three for eighteen Cucs, I paid twenty, and hoped the artisans were able to keep the extra for themselves.

Our tour picked up at the charming Galeria Carmen Montilla art gallery founded in 1994 in an old-fashioned 18th century colonial building that still has its original architecture but underwent restoration work following a fire in the 1980s. The gallery of the late Venezuelan painter, Carmen Montilla Tinoco, described as a great friend of Cuba, faces the San Francisco Convent. The lobby gallery opens to an interior courtyard filled with sculptures and an impressive ceramic wall mural. One mural, called "Flora and Fauna" by a local ceramist, hangs in the doorway of the patio. Many stone walls were made of sea urchins and shells that are distinctly visible in the rocks and felt rough when I brushed my arm while walking by too closely.

Most houses lining the avenue were painted in bright pastels: one pink with a green iron veranda, another blue with light blue decking, one pink with teal decking and one white with green shutters. The architecture reminded me of other colorful Caribbean and Central American sights I'd seen over the years. Another old square, once named for the church that formerly stood here, further highlights Cuban history. Originally called Plaza de Iglesia, it was renamed Plaza de Armas when a 16th century governor began using the square for military practices. Here we stopped at the booksellers and antiques shops.

The Church Tower at La Habana Cathedral has two tall clock towers flanking the entrance. Inside it smelled musty. The enormously tall and wide round columns of splotchy grayish-gold marble curved into the arched ceiling. The columns looked about the circumference of a giant redwood tree in northern California. It felt slightly cooler. At the front, hanging from the dome, dangled a chandelier of hundreds of glimmering crystals. I stood underneath gazing up then walked to the alter at the front looking at hand-painted pictures of saints. Stepping back, I spotted three little windows above the main alter. A ray of sunshine seeped through one window, struck a pew then spilled light onto the dusty floor. Off to the left stood an impressive full-size statue of a pope. Tourists were having their photos taken with him. I wanted to hang out longer in the natural air-conditioned building but the time had come to return to our home-away-from-home.

We returned to our floating hotel thoroughly entrenched in Old Habana history and after a leisurely casual dinner, I watched the sunset turn from auburn to scarlet and bronze before dipping into the ocean. As the city lights flickered on and off, the sixty-six-foot-tall white Jesus glowed awash in gleaming lights overlooking His city and a visitor, me. For some reason I felt welcome and secure knowing He was standing guard.

Habana - Day Dos

Adorned with a green circle #1, I climbed into our new, air-conditioned bus for a full day touring Habana. Yes! Tour group #1 today not #17. Carole Lee, Fran and I figured out the tour system and decided from then on we wanted to be with the first group out for the day, the rationale being it might be cooler in the morning than the afternoon. I quickly learned humidity knows no time. Equipped with my cross-over Baggalini purse hitting my left side, the water bottle holder with bottle hitting my other side, I certainly didn't look much like a tourist; right, not much.

The water bottle holder had been crafted of Alpaca wool carefully embroidered with blues, greens and teal colors, with the words Machu Picchu. I had purchased it six weeks earlier trekking through Peru and it had been the most useful purchase from that expedition. The holder, not me, had been attracting attention and conversation. Some years back I had been complimented by a man after organizing a weekend alumni reunion for two hundred fifty people when he said, "You're useful as well as ornamental." I felt the same way about my Peruvian bottle holder. One vendor asked to see it and took a picture. I had no doubt she would be crafting something similar in the near future and I fully expect to see hundreds of variations upon my return, hopefully in a few years.

I felt grateful. As a tourist I got to hop off and on the air-conditioned bus and knew I would return to our air-conditioned ship. I learned from our tour guide of the day, Ana, that the majority of Cubans have no AC in their homes. They could purchase a wall-unit for several hundred dollars when they saved enough money, but also then must pay the difference in electricity costs between what was already subsidized. Only a small percentage had air conditioning in only one room. She and her husband had just put one in their bedroom. Ana wore a white blouse with black slacks accented by a colorful scarf for a pop of color, adding her own personality or maybe making a personal statement. Her hair was black, her skin light brown with matching brown eyes and like Ernesto, a bright smile, but hers oozed an easiness and confidence.

Rarely did we hear honking horns because there weren't many cars. Cars are a luxury that most can't afford and with adequate transportation around the city and country, just not necessary. Driving down a fairly empty six-lane boulevard, our bus came to a stop at a light. Even with four streets emptying into the intersection, there were very few cars. Our bus sat behind a baby-blue-with-white-top Chevy pulling a pint-size trailer. Parked next to it was a hot pink Cadillac and in the third lane was a forest green

Rambler, all stopped next to each other at a stop light. They were evenly lined up and looked ready for a drag race but they weren't revving their motors like in the movies. Something moved in the back of the open-ended cart pulled by the Chevy. There were two pigs standing side-by-side plus other items crammed in around them. When the light switched to green, dark exhaust billowed from the tailpipes of the Caddy and Rambler as they slowly drove off.

Winding our way through the unjammed streets, we drove through a neighborhood. I wondered if the residents were getting used to seeing tour buses rambling through their avenues. We passed by women walking their children to school as our bus slowly pulled in alongside an entire block of murals painted on cement walls. We were visiting a neighborhood art exhibit called Muraleando. Several dozen singing and laughing youngsters dressed in matching beige and brown uniforms were just leaving after an hour music class. Many high-fived us as they strolled down the street back to their school. Ana explained that two local artists began teaching art workshops in the neighborhood school in 2001 and had no intention of starting a community development project. But their classes conflicted with the schedule of the state-run computer program so they moved the workshops into the streets, and there the seeds of Muraleando, meaning "muraling," began. The murals depict fanciful celebrations of Cuban life with dancers, singers, from children to seniors and stretched down the street and around the corner.

We climbed a mosaic-tiled, shiny stone staircase then entered into a multitiered tropical oasis filled with blooming flowers, tables scattered with artwork, and statues of whimsical characters, birds and butterflies. I walked down some stairs to a sunlit room where a young girl concentrated intently painting a red, yellow, pink and orange butterfly with dabs of green and blue on its wings and towing the Cuban flag like an airplane pulling a banner that might read "Will You Marry Me?" or advertising "Big Bargains at Withnell Motors" at home. Her painting included a swirly blue sky with puffy white clouds with some green and purple added for what reason, only the artist would know. Vertical grass-green soft lines with yellow highlights became the artist's ground. Her face lit up as two of us entered and asked if we could watch her. She shyly introduced herself as Laura and had Down Syndrome. Laura let me buy her painting and she signed it for me. It is proudly displayed in my home's Zen den and when I look at it, I am transported back to that time and place and sweet, smiling Laura.

Different rooms revealed diverse art. In a country where nothing is disposable and everything is useful, old manual typewriters and dial telephones, metal tire rims, bulbs and lights, wrought-iron chair parts, all were fair game to weld and paint and turn into unique and amazing sculptures of people, animals, flowers and many unrecognizable creations. We were escorted to the top level where a band and vocal group attempted to teach us some local songs and dances. After a mojito or two, many of us tried and all of us laughed.

Back on our panoramic tour of the city, the streets were dotted with bright orange-blossomed trees that we learned are actually called Flame Trees or Royal Poinciana. We drove up the famous Paseo del Prado and past Parque Central, and Gran Teatro de La Habana, home of the Cuban National Ballet, just reopened after a two-year restoration, and El Capitolio, the Capitol, now cloaked in wires for extensive renovation. We pulled into Revolution Square, not only a place for speeches and huge crowds but to show off one's snazzy car. Lined up down one side of the street sat a spotless cherry Chevy convertible, a fuchsia convertible of some kind, and a baby blue and white Mercury. Some were converted into taxis and tourists were squished in going for rides. I could hardly believe it—I was standing in the middle of the ginormous Revolution Square where not only had Cuban heroes and dictators spoken but two Popes and recently a U.S. president. Off the right shoulder of the monument statue of José Marti, the red, white and blue Cuban flag gently swayed in the breeze. At ten o'clock, in an already extremely warm, muggy morning even just standing still, I felt a trickle of sweat start at the top of my head, weaving its way down to my neck where I caught it with a tissue before it got any farther. I have never liked to sweat, especially my head, because it feels likes bugs in my hair. We really don't have many creepy-crawlies in the Pacific Northwest. So what? There I stood in Habana's Revolution Square, where thousands of others had stood for various causes. I wondered what my cause could, would or should be.

The cement Plaza, they were proud to tell, is the thirty-first largest city square in the world. It is notable for being where many political rallies took place and political figures addressed Cubans. Pope John Paul II, during his 1998 world tour, became the first pope to visit, and Pope Francis held large masses in the square in 2015. We were told that after Pope John Paul's visit Fidel allowed Christmas to become a national holiday. After Francis's visit Raúl declared Good Friday as a national holiday. Cubans like it when a pope visits. This historically significant square is dominated by the José Marti Memorial fifty-eight-foot statue, memorializing his commitment to and love for the people of Cuba. The National Library and many other government buildings flank the Plaza. Located behind the memorial is the Palace of the Revolution, the seat of the Cuban government and Communist party. We weren't invited in. Opposite the memorial are the offices of the ministries of the interior and communications, whose facades feature matching steel memorials of two of the most important deceased heroes of the Cuban Revolution, Ché Guevara and Camilo Cienfuegos. Camilo is often mistaken for Fidel Castro. There is an elevator with access to the top of the three hundred fifty-eight-foot memorial, one of the tallest points and best views in Habana, but it never works, our guide told us. As I stood there gawking, a shiny new red double-decker Habana Bus Tours drove by with a few riders scattered around the top deck, quite a contrast to the majority of the vehicles from the 1950s.

While strolling around the square, Ana shared privately with me that she loves her country and felt now she could speak openly as the government told the tour guides they could answer any questions asked. But she also knew her parents and others even older were afraid to talk openly. She explained that her age group was more hopeful than in her parents' era. Her parents were my age. She had been raised in the middle of the country halfway between Habana and Cienfuegos in the Matanzas region by her parents who were hardworking and motivated her to do as well as she could. They farmed the land, had one horse, and her father had been a teacher in an elementary school. Her mother stayed home while she and her two siblings were young. Her father had an old American car that he loved to tinker with and tried to keep running. He melted metal and then made parts when others were no longer working. He became well-known and loved working on cars more than teaching. It became time-consuming, so he started doing it full-time and evenings. He made more money than teaching and opened a little garage. When Ana and her brother and sister were in high school, her mother wanted to become a doctor so she left Cuba and went to an eastern European country where she studied and became a gynecologist. Her mother earned $30 per month working at a hospital in Habana. Her parents were considered well-off with a combined salary of $60 - $70 per month.

Ana's parents always wanted better for their children. Ana knew she had to strike out on her own so after four years of college furnished by the government, she went to work at the university as a teacher earning $13.50 per month. She subsidized that income by being a tour guide and within the last year or so, those working in the tourism industry were able to keep all their tips. She reminded me that their health care and all of her schooling had been provided through college but as a trade-off she did have to work for the government in a job that they told her to do for two years. She had been paid a salary and felt fortunate that they told her she had to be a teacher for two years, which she wanted anyway. She said it didn't usually happen that way. A person with an engineering degree might end up working in a store for two years. But after the two years, a person could find a job in their desired field, if it's available. And she had a ration book that charted her food supplies. This included one pound of meat per month. If she wanted to buy more, she could. She didn't have or need a car because transportation was adequate and a vehicle was too expensive. Her husband was a general doctor in a hospital and he made $25 per month.

Back with our group, Ana pointed out a compact Coco taxi, short for coconut because of its yellow spherical shape. Basically, the car was about the size of a Smart Car in Europe but made of fiberglass and plastic. There were hundreds of Coco taxis in Habana but only this city. The yellow ones were for tourists and black for locals.

We saw Ernest Hemingway's neighborhood and the 1817 pink two-story La Floridita Bar where he spent a lot of time, of course doing research for his writing. This area reminded me of my trip several years earlier to Key West and touring his home where the Hemingway house tour guide explained Ernest wrote six short story collections, seven novels and two nonfiction works. He produced most of his works between the mid-1920s through the mid-1950s and won the Nobel Prize in Literature in 1954.

I remembered that the Key West guide that told us that Ernest served in World War I and had been seriously wounded. His war experience became the basis for his novel, *A Farewell to Arms*, written in 1929. He had been married four times. Shortly after writing *The Old Man and the Sea* in 1952, he went to Africa on safari and almost got killed in two plane crashes that left him in pain or ill for much of his remaining life. He had permanent residences in Key West and Cuba, and bought a third house in Ketchum, Idaho, where he committed suicide. Additional works were published after his death. What a sad way to end such a unique life, I thought to myself.

Standing in front of the La Floridita Bar, Ana informed us that Ernest had been a main fixture of Habana and stayed in the country longer than many other Americans when relations between the two countries deteriorated. He fished extensively aboard his boat named Pilar, and enjoyed the island lifestyle, hanging out in Habana. In 1940 he and wife number three, Martha, purchased a home just outside Habana where they lived for two decades. They named their home, "Finca Vigía" or "lookout farm." They had many cats as well as trophies from many hunting and fishing expeditions. I remembered lots of cats at his home in Key West, supposedly descendants of his many felines.

For lunch at the La Criollo restaurant, another government establishment, we were escorted to tables in a covered outdoor area brimming with flowering bushes and shrubs. I could hear the familiar song of wrens and warblers but they were hard to find in the lush, thick trees and bushes. I spotted the Cuban Emerald, a typical bright green hummingbird, unfortunately not the one I hoped to see. I'd been watching and hoping to find a Bee Hummingbird, the smallest in the world, and when I asked if it might be possible, Ana said most birds were located in the interior of the country. While musicians strummed guitars (one strolled with drums tied around his waist, and a brightly dressed lady with maracas entertained us), we munched on crunchy thin breadsticks and drank complimentary minty mojitos. Piping hot plates full of mixed beans and rice were complemented by well-seasoned and flavorful pulled pork, mixed vegetables, and plantains, a member of the banana family. The final course emerged—a dense slice of bread or maybe thin cake soaked in some runny, syrupy sweet sauce. We tried everything, some food tasting better than others.

After lunch we drove along the seawall Malecón, a five-mile long esplanade, with expansive public space that runs along the northern rocky coastline. It separates Habana from the Straits of Florida and protects its northern coastline from potentially damaging ocean waves that threaten to jump the wall and overflow into the streets. The wide-open boulevard serves not only as a major traffic artery but also as a scenic venue where you can see ships entering the port of Habana. In a park stood a bronze statue of Maceo sitting tall astride his horse. Maceo fought in nine hundred battles and had been wounded twenty-five times. He became one of the most popular liberation army leaders during the country's Ten Years War for independence from Spanish colonial rule.

Fishermen were lined along the seawall and an Afro-Cuban woman was walking along the wide ledge gazing at the sea. As her black hair and white skirt blew in the wind, I pondered what she could be thinking. In front of us rumbled a purple Chevy convertible crammed with five passengers. The driver and one male passenger hung onto their straw hats, while in the backseat, the women's hair freely whooshed in the wind even though one lost her lime green scarf as the driver stepped on the gas and pulled out quickly. For some reason, the scene reminded me of a rerun of a 1950s Doris Day and Rock Hudson movie.

A fabulous vantage point appeared at the eastern end of Malecón where the channel tapers and separates Old Town from East Habana and provides a shipping lane from the Straits of Florida to the Bay of Habana. The channel is flanked by two forts, Castillo del Morro and Castillo de la Punta and across the bay was the gleaming white Jesus. Across the street was the boxy, unimpressive multistory new Embassy of the United States of America, a site still extremely unusual for Cubans according to Ana.

We drove across the bridge of the Almendares River. It is a twenty-eight-mile river that supplies water for Habana and part of the river forms the Metropolitan Park just a few miles upstream from the ocean. They are striving to maintain the old trees and other vegetation in conjunction with restoring Habana Bay, monitoring and controlling water pollution. Ana said that until two years ago, sewage poured directly into the Habana harbor. Yuck.

I took copious photos of cars: a Chevy Impala coated in three shades of green looked familiar, much like my husband's first car but his was silver; a red and white Buick Skylark with white tires; a black Packard that looked like somebody from the mob owned it; cars with tailfins with lots of shiny chrome that seemed to be from the space age; a yellow '57 Chevy reminded me of a high school boyfriend's first car but his was baby blue; a gray Dodge La Femme; a royal blue Edsel; a green Dodge Coronet two-door; a Nash Metropolitan white top. It was like an oldies car show in Las Vegas.

When I saw a shiny black Ford Fairlane, I had a flashback to my first car, a '64. I wanted to jump out of my seat on the bus and yell for the driver to stop but I didn't. I still miss that gem of a car and wished I'd never sold it to my younger brother forty years ago. The Cuban model was a two-door (mine was a four-door) but it had a red stripe down the side and I could even see the red steering wheel and red interior, but the wheels had spokes and the rear window had disappeared. After a short drive, we heard some secrets and lore at the one hundred forty-acre Cementerio de Cristobal Colon, where the same Carrara marble used here was used to create Jesus at the harbor. The avenues of marble walkways, monuments and elaborate Baroque-style mausoleums make this massive cemetery almost a ghost city of its own. I would never be able to even guess how much money had been spent there.

235

In the Museo Nacional de Bellas Artes (National Museum of Art), we climbed to the third level to view some depressing and sad pictures, an expression of those times. It appeared the artists didn't have any hope or joy in their lives. But each level we dropped, the artwork lightened and emerged more hopeful. On the ground floor pictures included landscapes, scenery, animals, children, butterflies and birds, in contrast to just two floors higher. Spanning five centuries, the art is witness to the important role arts have played in the Cuban culture. We saw the crumbling Old Wall of the city, visiting a craft market where I purchased four hand-crafted inlaid wood boxes for more than the asking price. I enjoyed the raised eyebrows when I told them to keep the change for themselves. I didn't want anyone to ever say about me what I'd heard unfortunately around the globe, the term "Ugly American." Single-handedly I tried to change it. We said farewell to Ana and I gave her a tip requesting she use it for something new for herself or maybe dinner at a restaurant with her husband. She gave me a stiff yet polite hug and wished me a happy life.

After dinner, back on Adonia, I stood on the deck waving goodbye to locals dotting the shoreline in their fishing boats and on docks as the persimmon-colored sun dropped lower in the sky. The sun looked sliced in half by a band of clouds before dropping entirely behind the cloud bank where I could see only uneven shards of silver strands before they plopped into the sea. That evening on the deck, comfy in lounge chairs with no blankets needed, we watched *The Old Man and the Sea*. This version had been filmed in 1958 in Cuba with Spencer Tracy. One of his most famous works, it tells the story of Santiago, an aging Cuban fisherman, who struggles with a giant marlin far out in the Gulf Stream off the coast of Florida. I felt mesmerized and along with the experiences of the day, it was a bit thought-provoking. And I could hardly wait to see what else I would be discovering.

Cienfuegos, La Perla Del Sur

I saw 6:37 on my clock Thursday morning as I hopped up early to watch another sunrise. The captain had told us the entrance to this city would be well worth the early rise. He guaranteed we wouldn't be disappointed as he would carefully guide us through S-curves around dozens of little islands. I quickly threw on light-weight cotton attire and for now, I had the entire top deck all to myself and noticed, because of the darkness, twinkling lights that reminded me of fireflies, blinking off and on. The sun rose over the sprawled-out town as the lightning bugs were extinguished. It gave the impression of peace and tranquility.

By now, I recalled something I'd learned on our first cruise through the Panama Canal. One's camera will not fog up due to humidity if you put it in a zip lock plastic bag for a few minutes and let it acclimate. My camera, now fog-less, was ready for photo ops.

Towards the middle of town, I could see a towering red-domed building that loomed over houses and buildings. We cruised by a bright blue two-story house with the sign of an anchor which I now knew indicated a room would be available for rent to a tourist—maybe Airbnb had arrived like in many other countries. Two men were standing on the deck waving. As we cruised into this city it looked like we were pulling into a neighborhood, not the typical industrial port area. A Cuban Parrot, bright green with pinkish red throat, circled as if he might be saying, "Take a good look at how handsome I am." My guess is he liked the air currents the ship generated but I felt grateful for his cooperation.

I walked through the entrance of a customs building that appeared more like a massive tipped-over cracker box. The walls were a glaring stark white due to the fluorescent tube lights with no covers over the fixtures to subdue the glare. I still don't know what the reason was for the need to determine a tourist's temperature but three men clad in white jackets pointed a gadget at each person's forehead. With no indication if I was fine or not, I walked on. Obviously, their methods were not as technically advanced like the hidden thermometers we knew were somewhere in the walls in the Habana pier terminal. This city is located in the central-south region of Cuba. The dock looked empty, unusual for a cruise ship terminal. I spotted a woman peddling a bike with probably her son on the back dressed in his brown school uniform.

Again, Carole Lee, Fran and I made it on bus #1 and our guide for this day introduced himself as Mario. He oozed poise with an easy swagger, seemed comfortable with leading a group of foreigners and was extremely good-looking, probably because of his constant tan, and dark and gentle but alert eyes. He seemed comfortable with his appearance and sure of himself. I would discover later that external looks could be deceiving when he opened up about some of his personal life and anecdotes.

Mario told us Cienfuegos (seein-fue-gos) had been established in 1819 by Frenchman Luis Declouet. I quickly saw that it appeared extremely different than Spanish-influenced Habana and why it is called the "Pearl of the South." Founded by French colonists, the city has straight streets and varied styles of buildings. In parks, plazas, structures and monuments I noticed neoclassical, art nouveau and art deco styles. Some buildings reminded me of the snazzy art deco buildings in South Beach, Florida that I saw a several years earlier with faux-nephew Grant.

Our first point of interest started at a daily market. I was struck with pungent aromas seeming to come from the stalls and tables full of grains, fruits and vegetables, and bread products. One long table displayed perfectly formed pyramids of yellow corn meal, white rice, brown and black beans. A boom box from somewhere in the middle of the building blared Cuban music, and across the street the Catholic church bells chimed nine times. Uncovered and unrefrigerated meats were being cut with a cleaver and measured using the metric system. This area seemed to be the culprit causing the odors. I saw "Hasta La Victoria Siempre" scrawled boldly on the wall and I asked Mario about it. He replied that this phrase had been used by Che Guevara as a sign-off on the letters to Fidel Castro during the Cuban revolution, meaning "Until we are victorious I remain always," or "Till victory forever!"

Loitering at the corner outside waiting for others to finish, I admired more colorful French architecture as across the street locals stood in line for public transportation. While wasting time before entering "La Purisima Concepción" (Saint Church Cathedral) as a group, a man probably in his mid-fifties wearing a light brown shirt including shoulder epaulets with two white stripes, and dark brown slacks, stopped and greeted me. He wore a pukka shell necklace tightly around his neck and a lanyard holding his official name badge. A brown baseball cap that read "Protecc…" (the rest of the letters were hidden on the other side) covered his head.

Except for his bright white smile and pukka necklace, his overall look appeared brown including his gentle, kind eyes. He said, "Good morning, I see you are from the ship," and laughed as he pointed to the #1 pink disk on my blouse. "I am on my way to my job where I work for the Department of Ministry. I wish to say thank you for coming to my country. We are happy to have you here and hope that our meetings like this will encourage our governments to be more open for us to get to know each other. This is an important time for my country and I am hopeful for great advances. Please encourage your friends in America to come. It is people like you and I who can make change happen. God bless you and please return." He spoke better English than many living in my home state and was clearly well-educated. I told him I truly appreciated his kind words and that he had stopped to talk to me. As I watched him walk down the street towards a government building he turned and waved, I waved back. I got teary about this serendipitous meeting and still am as I write this story today.

José Martí Park is considered one of the prettiest and well-preserved in Cuba. The government's palace with its huge red dome that I spotted as we cruised in that morning, the two-story Catalan-influenced Ferrer Palace with its exterior black spiral staircase leading to a dome-shaped vantage point, and the Teatro Tomas Terry Theatre from the 1890s, are next door neighbors to the Saint Church Cathedral.

The cathedral has asymmetric bell towers with matching red caps. We entered as a group but walked around at our own pace, stopping at different statues and naves. The inside smelled dusty, not a shock with the construction. Yet it seemed dull, and that surprised me. Most of the Catholic churches I had seen around the world were usually extravagant and magnificent. A slight but refreshing breeze found its way in from the plaza. White pillars and arches were striking but the stained-glass windows took the award with the designs, patterns and colors. With ongoing refurbishment and lack of finances, like many buildings in constant need of repair in Cuba, I wasn't surprised to find at the exit a fundraising poster that read "Together we contribute and build, meter by meter." One worker shared quietly that the restoration had been going at a snail's pace. Since I had worked in fundraising for thirty years, I gladly left a contribution to this important centerpiece of this pleasant town.

Different monuments and statues were scattered around the plaza like no one really planned it out.

One enormous, white marble lion had its left paw on top of a world globe. He looked a lot like Aslan from the C.S. Lewis *Chronicles of Narnia*. It appeared he might be contemplating crushing it or possibly trying to pick it up thinking he had the whole world in his hand?

"Fran, what do you think the lion is trying to depict?" I asked. But she didn't answer. One second Fran had been walking beside me and the next she had disappeared into thin air. Down several side streets were stalls of venders selling their handmade goods and wooden products in every shape possible including hand-carved replica cars painted in bright colors. A few minutes later, Fran reappeared at my side like she'd never been gone except her bag overflowed with newly purchased items. She reminded me of Road Runner in my childhood cartoons zooming around but without the special effects sounds. I bought five small carved houses each with a brightly painted front door for special friends at home, but I would keep one for myself.

Open arches led me down corridors of buildings lined with potted palms and birds and butterflies darting around. There were so many hummingbirds zipping around from one bush to the other, I was careful not to get buzzed in the head. One building had four doors all painted a different color—one blue as the sea water, one walnut brown, one sunshine yellow and the last one, fuchsia pink. My curiosity almost got the better of me but I didn't see one open, not even a crack. I lingered as long as I dared but saw no one come out. What would I find behind those colorful doors, secretly hoping my made-up word,

"Graviosity," would just happen? My word is a combination of gravity and curiosity; sometimes doors just magically open for me. In my head my husband's voice rang out loud and clear since he wasn't there to try to keep me in check: "Do not go anywhere you are not invited. Do not take a banner or flag or anything that doesn't belong to you. Do not push any buttons or pull any handles. Do not get arrested." He had watched news reports where stupid tourists had done even stupider things and were still experiencing communist hospitality and consequences in prison for their pranks and idiocy. No, I would not push open one of those beckoning colorful doors.

Walking beside me was a man carrying a warbling yellow canary in a wooden cage; its song was strong and loud with the several-note tweet. I greeted him and when I asked him about it he explained his bird liked to go on walks with him because it got him out in the fresh air and he was lonely by himself in their apartment. Seemed reasonable to me. I went in to what had been a Sears store before the embargo in the 1960s, and is now a department store with items made in Cuba, Russia and South America. I felt like I'd stepped back about five decades in time as it looked much like the Sears building in my childhood hometown.

We stopped at the Teatro Tomas Terry Theatre, a nine hundred fifty seat horseshoe-shaped theater finished in 1889 to honor Venezuelan industrialist Tomas Terry. A life-size statue of the dapper mustached Tomas proudly sits in a chair angled towards the front as if to welcome guests to his theater. The auditorium walls are awash in elegant French and

Italian architecture with Carrara marble, hand-carved Cuban hardwoods and quirky ceiling frescoes—some laughing, some crying and others with whimsical facial expressions I couldn't distinguish.

We heard a well-known á capella professional choir that serenaded us for forty-five minutes with local, traditional and some recognizable numbers. After the extraordinary concert in four-part harmony, we had the opportunity to hear directly from each singer as we peppered them with questions about their profession and art. They were all highly trained musicians and won many awards around the world in competitions. All had a second job as a music instructor, teacher or tutor in area schools.

The oldest member of our tour was a ninety-two-year old Navy veteran proudly wearing his Navy baseball cap. Even though using a walker and it being extremely warm, he did surprisingly well keeping up with our group. He shared with me that he felt emotional and was glad he'd come on this trip. He hoped other World War II veterans could make this journey. I told him about my father being in the 10th Mountain Division serving in Italy. He said those Army guys really had it bad in Europe and he'd spent his time floating around the South Pacific on a ship. I chuckled and said my ninety-five-year-old father-in-law had served in the Navy also but I knew they hadn't had it easy either.

The drive along the coastline revealed homes of various styles and colors with black iron fences and broken brick walkways. A worker balanced on rickety iron rods, not scaffolding, sat on a thin wooden slab stretching arms length replacing a bulb on a streetlight. We drove by Fidel Castro's home, an unpretentious sprawling ranch-style wooden house.

The word "Revolucion" appeared often, painted randomly on the cement walls that separated the sidewalks from the private property. Makeshift soccer fields were in neighborhoods. We drove by the baseball stadium complete with its own full-scale cement elephant on a grassy area at the front entrance. Mario explained the Cienfuegos team is part of the Cuban National Series and the nickname is the Elephants, his team, created in 1977. He shook his head as he said they had their best season their second year of existence, finishing fourth in the National Series. They have never come close to replicating that success. We drove down the Malecón, a boulevard lined with stately homes, old hotels, neoclassical buildings with pastel-painted columns, homes with rooms to rent; every building had a view of the sea.

At the intersection of Avenue 54 we met Benny Moré, or rather a statue of the famed Salsa singer, a six-foot man cast in bronze but not hoisted up on a typical pedestal. Instead he strides in walking position completely stationary on the most bustling corner of Cienfuegos. Benny sports a broad-brimmed hat, carries his cane, and wears baggy clothing with bright shiny shoes, mostly from people rubbing them that way. Mario told us that Benny was one of eighteen children and is often referred to as the greatest Cuban singer of all time. Benny combined Afro-Cuban and Spanish-derived music of the Cuban countryside knowing both the African and European elements of Cuban music. It allowed him to be comfortable in all different styles. Known for his talent with boleros, mambos and rhumbas, he also conveyed a tenderness and emotional appeal through his singing and dancing. After being discovered, he traveled to Mexico but returned to Cuba in 1953. Though he could not read music, he composed two of his smash hits. He had been a bandleader and assembled a powerful big band comprised of talented musicians. He didn't live long because of his love for rum. He died of cirrhosis of the liver in 1963. It seemed clear, even though in his thirties, Mario was a big Benny fan.

Across from Benny, people were shopping at a store using their ration books. A girl about six years old dressed in a lime green summer top with matching green skirt, held hands with her dad who wore jeans and a plaid blue and white shirt. They, along with most others, dressed in western-world style clothing.

Earlier on the bus, Mario had passed around his ration book and there were marks and dates in straight columns indicating he'd picked up his allotted amount for that week. The words were in Spanish, which I couldn't translate, but he told us the items were beans, rice, staples like flour and corn meal, cereals, milk, bread, fruits and vegetables. Going into the government ration store we saw aisles full of items but no variety or choices, only one type of tissue, one type of diapers, toilet paper and towels. Basics were provided with no frills.

Before we were delivered back to the ship, Mario shared a story with us during the drive time that simultaneously had the entire busload of tourist laughing and shaking our heads. He owned a 1978 Russian motorcycle that he used as his transportation and it kept breaking down. He said he wanted to purchase a new one but the cost would be around $8,000. According to his calculations he'd be seventy years old before he could afford it, making less than $20 per month. He mentioned that being a college graduate didn't guarantee any type of a well-paying job. Even though his college education had been free of charge, he was in turn required to work two years where the government sent him. He was assigned to a store selling clothing; he seemed perturbed and obviously felt he had more potential. He told the story of trying to get his motorcycle registered in the name of his new wife so she could legally drive it too. Every time he went to the government office to attempt the process, something was wrong on the form he had completed. Repeatedly there appeared to be new and different issues he hadn't encountered previously. It took three years to get her name on the title of his motorcycle. By that time they were divorced. He really had us chuckling and said, "I tell you no lie, three years." He had chosen to leave her name on the title. Mario sort of chortled but also shook his head as he recounted his story to us. He said it was typical government. A man sitting across the aisle mumbled, "His story makes me feel slightly better about our DMV." I replied, "Absolutely, and I'll remember his saga next time I have to renew my driver's license."

We drove through uncrowded streets back to the ship. Saying thank you to Mario, we said farewell to this lovely city. As Adonia departed, in the trees along the shoreline we saw about a dozen roosting

White Ibis completely white except for red starting around their eyes to the tips of their curved bills and long bony legs. The S-curves made for a lengthy departure and I got to see it all in reverse and in the daylight instead of the semi-darkness of that morning. A two-story ferry went by packed with people, and now the norm, most were taking photos and waving. On the top uncovered deck sat a brown large-patterned floral sofa and matching chair; obviously, the ferry served as a delivery boat, too. A couple swimming waved. A well-worn dock held four people and a barking dog that looked like a coyote or scrawny German Shepherd. They all hollered and waved. Not far from them in the reeds were two stocky Green Herons and twice as tall, one Great Blue Heron with a small fish in its mouth.

The ferry pulled up to a sign-less dock and, as people started filing off, two men pushed the floral sofa over the edge of the top floor down to two men below who caught it and carried it off. The same process was used for the matching chair. As we passed a gray navy ship, one lone man was rowing and fishing in a dinghy; I can't call it a boat. He had a camera but didn't wave. He had his hands full with rowing and trying to take pictures at the same time.

Around one island there stood a hot pink painted house and out in front grew a bushy vibrant orange Flame Tree, a vivid display of brightness. Looking more closely at their makeshift dock, I saw no wooden planks to walk on but instead tree stumps with logs affixed in between. Each stump held its own Brown Pelican with its goldish, orange head shimmering in the light, looking for its fish dinner;

they seemed the only ones not interested in a cruise ship.

From the tenth floor of my floating hotel, I peered down on three-story rooftop decks and houses with roofs of varying colors and disrepair. I spotted the forts, bars and restaurants lining the bay as we cruised by saying farewell to the Pearl of the South. Several large brownish-black birds with narrow wings and forked tails, called Magnificent Frigatebirds, skimmed the top of the water snatching their evening dinner while escorting us out to sea.

Santiago de Cuba

On Friday morning, another new town loomed in the distance. Once again, I watched the sun come up from the ship's top deck, as we entered what had been the capital of the Spanish colony of Cuba from 1522 to 1589. Two men were standing on top of a garage taking pictures. They waved and I waved back. Towering red-and white-ringed smokestacks puffed out black smoke into the early morning blue sky. Fishermen in small boats were already busy casting their lines and three pelicans perched on the bobbing red buoy created by our wake. Electrical lines from each side of the harbor were held up by one lone tower on a small grassy island off to the left. I didn't think the ship's smokestack would fit under the lines. It did. A black Neotropic Cormorant, with a patch of yellow and brown at its throat, flew by and joined the pelicans on the crowded buoy.

As we got closer the roadways appeared empty. At eight o'clock I assumed many would be on their way to work. The day before, cruising at sea enjoying

249

classes, swimming and relaxing, we were warned that Santiago would be the hottest spot in the country. Sweat is sweat and we were all in it together, locals and tourists. It's the second largest city in Cuba and the capital of the southeastern province. It is considered to be the birthplace of "revolucion," where the watchtowers and cannons used in the Spanish-Cuban-American War still guard the city.

Score! Bus #1 again in hopes of beating the heat. Wrong. The humidity felt like the sauna at our gym. But it didn't matter. I stood in yet another town in Cuba hopefully encountering more new friends. Police on motorcycles were loitering, awaiting our arrival. I questioned silently if they thought we were a disruption, an intrusion or a positive element. Did Cubans feel suddenly like they were living in a fish bowl? I pondered how they might feel about all these tourists taking photos of them like we'd never seen a human being before. Then I recalled my years of photo taking, many of people—why did I think they were so different than me? Epiphany: I should stick to architecture, scenery and food photos.

We were warmly greeted and welcomed by our middle-aged guide, Felix. He seemed about four inches taller than me, stocky build, darker complexion than our previous guides and dapper in his snappy uniform. He was already applying his handkerchief liberally on his face and neck. He lives in Santiago, with a wife and a son who attends high school. Their daughter lives in Miami with her husband and five-year-old granddaughter. A professsor at the university, Felix also teaches English, which he spoke exceedingly well.

As we started our one-day tour, Felix told us about many famous people who came from Santiago de Cuba: Desi Arnaz, television actor and band leader in his role as Ricky Ricardo married to Lucy, of the *I Love Lucy* fame; other well-known names like Bacardí, the rum manufacturer; and famous baseball players, musicians and journalists.

We drove about six miles southwest of the city center in our air-conditioned bus led by our motor-cycle police escort, passing trucks loaded with people, horse-drawn wagons, mothers walking their children to school and lots of construction due to the devastation of Hurricane Sandy a few years earlier. Felix told us the motorcycle escort would ease our way through the traffic of which I saw little. I felt guilty and even more conspicuous in our big motorcoach when the police escort flipped on his siren to move very few people out of our way. We weren't that special to take priority over people living their everyday lives.

Rays of morning sun ricocheted off the crystal clear blue ocean like thousands of sparkling cut dia-monds as we drove up a winding road to Castillo de San Pedro de la Roca (Morro fort). The ten-minute stroll up the walkway to the castle was lined with thriving leafy bushes and loaded with purple hibiscus and other flowers I didn't recognize. Several differ-ent butterflies were flitting from bush to bush. I couldn't find the name of a petite bright green one in my guide book. I saw a Sleepy Orange, bright orange with a black swath at the top of its wings. There were several Nickerbean Blue butterflies of soft blue, almost a light gray, with two orange splotches and several black dots on their tails. But they never settled enough for me to get photos.

On our walk to the multilevel stone fort built into the rocky cliff, Felix explained the city's colonial past—this coastal fortress had been constructed in 1637 to protect Santiago de Cuba. I walked across the waterless moat and inside where a guide showed us well-preserved swords, guns and knives.

Exiting to explore on my own, I heard angelic music wafting around me. But I couldn't find immediately where the sounds were coming from because it bounced around several hundred-year-old stone walls. I wound down uneven stone blocks with no handrails, following the melodic sounds to a dinky chapel on the ground floor where four women all dressed in white, form-fitting long dresses, sang á capella. Along with two others, I stood there in reverent silence as the singers' voices blended effortlessly and ricocheted around the chapel as they sang *Nobody Knows*. One woman sang the low part and it transported me momentarily to three years earlier when I toured Oak Alley Plantation outside of Charleston, South Carolina. I witnessed a slave re-enactment and a woman singing the same song. A cool shiver ran down my spine and it wasn't perspiration. The Cuban quartet was called "Vidas." I made a contribution and got their CD—a perfect souvenir from this historic monument.

I climbed around the stone fort looking down the barrel of cannons and through peep holes etched in the thick walls where rifles one time were pointed to shoot at pirates or other intruders. Discovering a boulder with a fairly flat top I sat dangling my feet. I could see down the white sand beaches in both directions and at endless aqua water, changing to teal, then eventually to sapphire blue, the deeper the water became. A flock of large birds was diving into the water catching their morning feast. A jet flew overhead and I realized it had been the first one I noticed all week.

On a panoramic drive through the city, we passed by its most famous attraction, San Juan Hill. I didn't realize that the war actually had been fought across many of the hills that ring Santiago. On the eastern side, these highlands include a series of hills that are known as the San Juan Heights. American troops stormed what they saw as a central point of the fortifications on those heights. The point of that assault has come to be known as "San Juan Hill." I could almost picture, from reading my Cuban history books on my flight, Teddy Roosevelt and his Rough Riders, the Buffalo Soldiers of the 10th Cavalry and 24th Infantry Regiments, who did the heaviest fighting. Spanish General Linares ordered seven hundred sixty Spanish Army regular troops to hold the San Juan Heights against an American offensive on July 1, 1898. For unclear reasons Linares failed to reinforce this position, choosing to hold nearly ten thousand Spanish reserved in the city. A company from the Signal Corps ascended in a hot air balloon to scout the hills. It made for good target practice for the Spaniards.

Felix pointed out that the road we were driving on across San Juan Heights was just south of where the major assault occurred. The northern area of the Heights is now covered by residences and an apartment complex. He said that on one street corner one block north of the parkway there is a single small monument honoring the Rough Riders. Aside from that, there is little other evidence of military history.

Memorials to the war are near the center of the San Juan Heights. San Juan Hill is just the name that survives in American culture as the high point of the war. San Juan Hill, as we think of it, is really San Juan crest and became the center of war tributes. Today it is a popular public park. A school had been built (which became a hotel near the area), a zoo and an amusement park. It seemed odd to see a modern Ferris wheel, even though it doesn't work, towering above the historical memorials. Grassy areas preserve traces of trenches, old cannons are scattered throughout military monuments, and a large memorial structure honors fallen U.S. soldiers.

We drove by the Palace of Justice and Antonio Maceo Revolution Square, filled with enormous gray sculptures, towering gray columns and cement gray monuments. The multiple Cuban flags added the only color except for the green grass. At the Plaza de Marte, also called The Square of Liberty, located on one of the most central and highest points of the city, there is a tall white column for Los Veteranos, the veterans, that represents the independence and sovereignty of the Republic. There are many other statues and monuments of important people Cubans pay tribute to along with colorful buildings lining the square. Slow-moving, non-mufflered red, green or blue trucks, instead of buses, unloaded people into the bustling square.

We drove by the baseball stadium where the Wasps were league champions eight times between 1980 and 2008. Felix remains a true fan and hopes for better days for his team. The street has displays honoring local heroes, newly constructed brightly painted apartment buildings and porches strung with laundry from pillar to post. We drove the entire circumference of the Moncada Quarter (now a school), a Grey Poupon mustard-colored building, complete with bullet holes for emphasis of past troubled times. It was in the same neighborhood where yellow cranes were hoisting square cement blocks that would become someone's next home. Many were placed right next to a house that had fallen down. People scooted around on motorcycles, and canvas-topped bicycles towed a small cart or wagon usually filled with fruits or vegetables. It wasn't uncommon to see a 1950s Chevy, a horse pulling a wagon or a bike pulling a cart, next to each other parked at a traffic light.

We entered Santiago de Cuba Cathedral or Our Lady of Charity. Blessed Mary holds the Christ child and holds a crucifix atop an upside down crescent moon with three cherubs covered with jewels and golden crown and halo, like an embroidered gold crown, with the Cuban flag.

Just a quick drive from downtown we made it to the changing of the guard at Santa Ifigenia Cemetery where Cuban National Hero Jose Martí was laid to rest. The trio of guards dressed in military drab green exited a building and stepped high with exaggeration almost perfectly synchronized while tinny sounding recorded music blared through loud speakers. The trio joined two guards at the entrance for pomp and tradition. Martí's memorial is placed in such a fashion that during the daytime a beam of sunlight is always on it. And if it rains, he is above it. Several shrines to members of the Bacardi rum family were prominently displayed.

We were in for another new experience for lunch at Tré a Santiago Restaurante, a family-owned eatery instead of a government-run restaurant. I peeked at the dinky kitchen on the ground floor before we walked up one flight of stairs. With not much prep space, a four-burner stove and oven, and standard size refrigerator—could our lunch be coming from such a small place? The second-floor terrace had seating for about twenty-five with a view over-looking the city. The entire family of nine greeted us and sang a rousing song accompanied by a guitarist. The patio was adorned with brightly colored decora-tions and the tables were laid out in red and blue tablecloths. My roommate thought it was lovely that they were honoring us with the colors of our American flag but I knew the red, white and blue colors were also the hues of their flag. Cheery hand-painted tile murals of scenery and flowers were on the walls.

Friendly waiters delivered family-style plates of the first course—perfectly rounded melon balls linked by toothpicks. The next course was trays of deep fried vegetables and a sweet, spicy red sauce for dipping. Then came bowls of rice and beans mixed together. Deep fried shrimp, sautéed chicken and pork were deposited on our table on oval platters. A salad of greens and tomatoes with julienned carrots and no dressing turned up. And finally, a cake soaked in a light caramel sauce with colored sprinkles on top. Of course, the national drink, mojito, again magically, and marvelously, materialized. This was a frequent and welcomed happening.

The owner gave us a quick cooking class explaining that root vegetables are most often flavored with mojo, a combination of olive oil, lemon juice, onions, garlic and cumin. Hot spices are rarely used in Cuban cooking. The most common meals include those made with pork, chicken, rice, beans, tomatoes and lettuce. Fried or grilled chicken and grilled pork chops are typically eaten. Beef and seafood are rarely prepared with the exception of lobster which is so popular that it is becoming endangered in Cuba. Other common dishes are: ajiaco (typical meat and vegetable stew), fufú (boiled green bananas mashed into a paste) which is often eaten alongside meat, empanadas de carne (meat-filled pies or pancakes), and peccadillo (a snack of spiced beef, onion, and tomato). Ham and cheese are common as stuffing for fish and steaks or are eaten alone. Popular desserts are helado (ice cream), flan (baked custard), chu (bite-sized puff pastries with meringue) and churros (deep-fried doughnut rings).

I asked Felix if he would join me for lunch, guessing he might be about my age. I lowered my voice and I asked if he remembered the Cuban Missile Crisis, not sure if we should really talk about it. He did but is two years younger than me so he had been in the first grade. His two-years older sister and the rest of his family talked about it in their home. He remembered they were frightened but his parents comforted them saying they had survived worse times and this would be no different. Had I over-thought about Cuban children my age during the Missile Crisis and what they would have known or remembered? My remembrances weren't as clear as my parents' but Felix said no one in that age group would speak with me about it out of their traditional fear of consequences or having never learned Eng-lish. So, I decided to be satisfied with the experience of Felix knowing that we all did survive.

After profusely thanking our hosts, I left a tip in a clear jar hoping others would follow. They did. I had learned how much a dollar meant to these people. The meal we had just eaten would cost around seven to nine Cucs, or more, since we had shrimp. Most Cubans don't make that much money in one month. At home, it would have been a $15 lunch.

On the way to our next destination we drove through a neighborhood where tucked away between two buildings I saw a man working on an old car in a one-stall garage. Two younger men were leaning against a wall watching. One had a head of red hair with a scruffy mustache that hid his upper lip—he seemed out of place with his fair complexion. I decided he could be a descendent of the O'Reilly clan of Habana.

We were treated to a drama and musical presentation at Cutumba Ballet Folklorico. Could a ballet in Salsa be real? I'd seen the Bolshoi Ballet performed in St. Petersburg, Russia, and one in Portland, Oregon, and now my third ballet would be a total opposite of the first two. Seven women wore sleeveless, scooped-neck, calf-length, pattern-less

258

flowing dresses with matching head scarves. Two women were in red, three in blue and two in yellow. Twirling themselves with arms spread holding the hem of their dresses, each looked like a spinning fan; the colors melded together like a kaleidoscope. Along with three men dressed in all white with royal blue and red scarves, they combined song with bongos and drums, and acted out a story where the women always win! This renowned folkloric group, Cutumba, researched and collected histories of songs and stories and presented Afro-Franco-Haitian-Cuban origins found primarily in eastern Cuba. They were informative representatives of their Afro-Cuban culture and had been on several international tours throughout Europe, the Caribbean and South America.

After the upbeat and inspiring presentation, I strolled around the colonial buildings in Céspedes Park in the central square of Old Town. A man dozing on a park bench in the shade of a tree had his Panama hat covering his face next to the statue of the famous founding father, Carlos Manuel de Céspedes, of the Cuban independence in 1868. Carlos continues to gaze and watch over his people in his park, sleeping or otherwise.

We stopped by the Casa de la Cultura Miguel Matamoros, where Fidel gave his famous speech on January 1, 1959, declaring the triumph of the Revolution. The neoclassical city hall building at the northern end of the square was built in the 1950s but looks like a design from the 1700s. There were several arched openings on the ground floor and majestic blue, uniquely carved wooden doors at each entrance on the second floor. I sat and watched a dozen or so Yellow and Magnolia Warblers drink out of the turquoise fountain. They appeared similar to our goldfinches that gobbled tons of seed from our backyard feeders at home. The Square seemed a melting pot mix of talking, walking and guitar strumming.

To my left stood the oldest building in town, the newly renovated past residence of Diego Velázquez, the first governor of Cuba. Now it's used by vendors, taxis and entertainers. Just like in Habana, hanging overhead on wires were photos taken of several old historic buildings opposite the remodeled, refreshed versions of today.

Saying farewell to Felix was hard for me, especially after hearing a bit about his life and what I consider personal hardships due the inability to freely see his daughter and granddaughter who live in Miami. For several years he had saved the equivalent of the necessary two hundred dollars. He finally was given an appointment time to be interviewed at length at the U.S. Customs Office only to have the customs representative deny his VISA with no explanation and no refund. With a firm hand, she stamped DENIED on his paperwork. He was stunned and heartbroken, and went outside and cried. We encouraged him to try again but that kind of money is much more difficult for a Cuban to come up with than for us. I felt the saddest I had the entire trip. Even though he was a very upbeat person with a positive and hopeful outlook, to me he seemed slightly distrusting, like his hopes had been dashed too often.

We returned to the ship and the engines kicked in as we cruised slowly out of Santiago. Several motionless cars and trucks lined the edge of the curvy street stretching up a hill. People were hanging out of windows, standing atop their vehicles with cameras taking pictures of us and our ship. I recalled we were just the third group to visit their country, and to see a cruise ship must have been quite out of the ordinary for them. Then a sunshine yellow, four-door car stopped in the middle of the road. Following closely was a truckload of people now blocking more vehicles behind them. Three men stood in front of an old green station wagon, each with a hand shading his eyes from the sunshine, much like a baseball cap would have done. They enthusiastically waved and one jumped up and down. It appeared that they were trying to get my attention. They did. These three adults appeared childlike in their visible delight. Throughout the week, waves of different emotions poked my heart. This one jabbed hard. It dawned on me that I was in awe of the Cuban people and their sheer fortitude. I could never relate to their daily lives and what they had tolerated and experienced.

Perched in thick trees were large white birds, clearly not the White Ibis I'd spotted leaving Cienfuegos. These were storks according to the ship's staff standing at the railing beside me. Several were gliding in flight, circling around their winged friends in the trees below. Carefully, Adonia eased around the curves created by islands and land. The familiar red buoy I saw bouncing in the water that morning revealed only one egret. A butterfly fluttered and landed on the ledge right by me. The coloring looked more like a moth but my guidebook proved it to be a

Cuban Crescent with multiple brown tones with cream and white. I knew it was my sign that I should return one day. As emotional as I already felt about this trip of discovery and enlightenment, I knew the butterfly's appearance was encouraging me to tell its story and hurry back.

Now a familiar occurrence, people poured out of their homes, garages and businesses watching our exit including six boys and one girl on a cement dock all waving farewell. I waved back as enthusiastically as they did and I felt melancholy that I had to leave.

There seemed to be so much more to learn. I felt totally inconsequential as we cruised by Morro Fort that we had visited just that morning. Not knowing why I was feeling insignificant I thought to myself that maybe even I could make a difference by helping in some small way. But even after spending four days in this country, I didn't know exactly what. Yet. As I stood spying caves in the rocks that linked rough stairways to entrances from the water level that might have led invaders closer than they should have gotten, I daydreamed how I could smuggle goods to the sisters or Maria or Felix. Maybe I was meant to be a pirate.

That evening eight travel agents gathered for dinner and we shared that day's incidents and people we'd encountered. We all had different experiences to reveal. I started a list of "How To's" for the next trip and what to share with those intrepid explorers coming for the first time.

Three things happened during my four-day visit in the summer of 2016: Americans were now free to wander and visit with Cubans instead of staying with an organized group; six U.S. airlines were granted permission to fly to Cuba; and Cuban coffee beans could be purchased in the U.S. routed through some other foreign distributor. Hopefully, a beginning.

On our day at sea, I attended a class on sharing your story and one woman said, "We travel not to escape life but for life not to escape us." Another said, "Travel is more than seeing sights; it's a change that goes on within you, deep and everlasting." I fervently and adamantly agreed.

I loved what Mark Twain said, "Twenty years from now you will be more disappointed by the things you didn't do than the ones you did do. So throw off the bowlines, sail away from the safe harbor, catch the trade winds in your sails. Explore. Dream. Discover."

On that final day heading back to Miami, I wrote a postcard to my future self, reminding myself not to forget Felix and his story about trying to visit his daughter and granddaughter in Miami and the horrible experience he had with the U.S. customs representative. I hoped he would try again and again, if necessary, and never give up. With my new friends Carole Lee, and Fran, we recapped our incidents and encounters, and newly gained insight from the past week, especially our quick four days immersed in Cuban culture.

My hope is that humanitarian issues are addressed and resolved and that Cuba doesn't become westernized too quickly and can keep its uniqueness by not becoming just another Caribbean island. Both of my comrades agreed. I didn't miss seeing a Starbucks, McDonalds or KFC on every corner. It certainly didn't seem Cuba lacked its own eating establishments. There are not many places left in the world where an American can step back in time to an era with 1950s and early '60s vehicles and with no fast food restaurants or chain stores, and whichever political party is in control in our country that the progress started by President Obama continues. Change for change's sake is not a constructive step but changes that are well thought out would benefit all. But that's my perspective. A Cuban's perception is much different, I learned, as they see any type of change as progress and change is what they want. I agree that anyone deserves a decent wage. They should have the freedom to travel and return freely. And ending the economic embargo would be a colossal leap for the people of Cuba. I hope I am able to return and look forward to seeing what has changed with the sisters, and Ernesto, Ana, Mario and Felix.

I remembered hearing astronaut Neal Armstrong while watching our black and white television as a child, when he took the first steps on the moon in 1969. He said, "That's one small step for a man, one giant leap for mankind." I doubt Cuban children my age saw the same television coverage I did in 1969, but it seems like this statement might hold true for those living in Cuba in 2016.

Trip Tips:

Don't forget items in your carry-on for your long flight like earplugs or noise cancelling headphones, inflatable pillow, sanitizing wipes, compression socks, sleep aids, food, pen, paper and notepad or journal, chewing gum and one set of extra clothing. Don't forget your prescription medications.

Don't forget a plug adapter as most hotels use two-pronged 220V outlets (unless you're on a cruise ship).

Don't forget your passport and make a copy to put somewhere else in your luggage. Make a copy to leave at home with a trusted friend or relative.

Don't drink the water. Buy bottled and keep yourself hydrated and, if not on a cruise ship but in a hotel, use it to brush your teeth, too. And take a water bottle holder.

Don't go without a hand-held fan or buy one immediately upon arrival. Take tissues for a variety of uses.

Don't be shy, try a few words: Hello "Hola." Bye "Adios." How are you? "Cómo estás?" Study up on Spanish 101. Try to be a traveler not a tourist.

Don't expect air conditioning and if you are lucky enough to find a hotel with this extravagance, don't ask why it's not running or why it's not cold.

Don't be a show-off. Be modest and don't bring your expensive jewelry—less temptation and respecting that the average wage is $15 per month.

Don't take pictures of police or soldiers. It's illegal to take a photograph of any military, police or airport personnel. Always ask if you can take a photo, especially of children.

Don't overdo it on rum. It's plentiful and cheap but you don't want to reinforce the loud, ugly American reputation. Or get arrested.

Don't be finicky about the food; it's delicious and flavorful.

Don't forget some condiments like ketchup, jams, cinnamon and peanut butter if you can't live without them for a week or so. Many of these aren't available in Cuba but you can bring your own (probably not in your carry-on).

Don't speak badly of deceased Fidel. He was revered by many and they haven't been raised with freedom of speech. Remember what your mother said, "If you can't say something nice, don't say anything at all."

Don't blow your nose in public. They consider it crass so if you have a cold, excuse yourself and take care of things in private. Same thing for spitting in the streets, something most civilized people find disgusting.

Don't forget to bring a few little gifts: pencils, post-cards, pens, small hotel-size toiletries, pins with U.S. flags, even some t-shirts in good condition for ex-changes. Anything that reads USA, your home state, sports teams or flag will be highly sought after.

Don't forget that tipping is socially accepted and a polite practice to tip your wait staff, tour guides, hotel staff or bartender for good service. They get to keep their tips and an extra few dollars means a lot.

266

Don't assume you are being offered a free gift if someone offers to draw caricatures or poses for pictures.

Don't forget to count the change. Cucs are the new tourist currency that most foreign visitors use. The Cuban dual currency seems to be confusing to some travelers. Cuban currency is NOT traded internationally, so you can't buy it in advance. You buy it when you arrive in Cuba. Bring Euros, Canadian Dollars or Pounds Sterling with you for an easy and quick exchange into Cucs. If you exchange the U.S. Dollar there is both a tax and a commission charged, resulting in a devaluation of your money. The U.S. is the only country that gets hit with an extra ten percent penalty. This means $100 USD equals 87 Cucs. And only exchange at a bank or pier, never on the streets or in stores. You will need coins to use some restrooms.

Don't bother with plastic. In fact, any U.S. bank card currently won't work. This could change, but for now, cash is king.

Don't take unlicensed taxis. Agree on rates beforehand, just to be safe.

Don't order a "papaya" daiquiri. It's not the word daiquiri but the word "papaya" that is extremely offensive and a vulgar slang for female anatomy. The delicious fruit was renamed "fruta bomba," so when you're at a corner fruit stand or bar call it "fruta bomba" or just point.

Don't expect punctuality. Cuban time is similar to Hawaiian time or relaxed time. However, if your taxi ride is one hour, it will be one hour.

267

Don't skimp on supporting the local economy. High-quality, handcrafted giftware is plentiful. Pay the price and don't dicker; in fact, give them a little bit more. Reinforce that Americans are good-hearted and helpful. Even though our governments don't agree, we are people helping people. Do take a tote bag for shopping as many places don't have plastic bags. Make sure your treasures are made in Cuba and not Russia.

Don't forget to keep $25 handy. If you have flown in and are flying home, you will be asked to pay a $25 tourist departure tax upon leaving. Airports only take cash. This is not unusual; many countries have this tax.

Don't go in the summer. It will be hot and extremely humid. The locals sweat, too, but not as much as you will.

Don't be nervous to reach out and touch someone. Shake hands. A touch on an arm or a pat on the back will go a long way with new friendships. Smiles make the difference in starting all conversations.

Don't ask a question before a greeting. Don't walk into a store and ask, "Where is the toilet?" Walk in smiling and say, "Hola, good day, I am wondering if you could please point me to the toilet?" And be sure to say "Gracias." Pleasantries will always get you further than abruptness.

Don't worry about using your cell phone or the lack of Wi-Fi. If you plan on trying to find and use the internet you may be disappointed as it is highly regulated and rather expensive. You may need a special permit to access the internet, and even then, usage is closely monitored and spotty. It's changing too. If cruising, you may or may not find the ship's Wi-Fi to your satisfaction.

And lastly, remember to check government websites before you go for the latest rules and regulations because things change unexpectedly.

"Travel opens your eyes and your heart."

Deleen Wills

Made in the USA
Monee, IL
20 March 2021

62500316R00154